First World War
and Army of Occupation
War Diary
France, Belgium and Germany

57 DIVISION
Headquarters, Branches and Services
Adjutant and Quarter-Master General
2 February 1917 - 25 June 1919

WO95/2967/2

The Naval & Military Press Ltd
www.nmarchive.com
Published in association with The National Archives

Published by

The Naval & Military Press Ltd

Unit 10 Ridgewood Industrial Park,
Uckfield, East Sussex,
TN22 5QE England
Tel: +44 (0) 1825 749494

www.naval-military-press.com
www.nmarchive.com

This diary has been reprinted in facsimile from the original. Any imperfections are inevitably reproduced and the quality may fall short of modern type and cartographic standards.

© **Crown Copyright**
Images reproduced by permission of The National Archives, London, England, 2015.

Contents

Document type	Place/Title	Date From	Date To
Heading	WO95/2967/2 57 Division HQ Branches Services Adjutant QM General Feb 1917-June 1919		
Heading	57th Division "A" & "Q" Branch Feb 1917-Jun 1919 1917 Feb-1919 Jun		
War Diary	Boulogne	02/02/1917	02/02/1917
War Diary	Bailleul	03/02/1917	03/02/1917
War Diary	Sailly Sur Lys	04/02/1917	13/02/1917
War Diary	Merris Area	14/02/1917	16/02/1917
War Diary	Bailleul	17/02/1917	17/02/1917
War Diary	Merris Area	17/02/1917	18/02/1917
War Diary	Sailly	18/02/1917	18/02/1917
War Diary	Merris Area	19/02/1917	19/02/1917
War Diary	Sailly	20/02/1917	21/02/1917
War Diary	Merris	21/02/1917	21/02/1917
War Diary	Sailly	22/02/1917	23/02/1917
War Diary	Merris	24/02/1917	24/02/1917
War Diary	Sailly	25/02/1917	31/03/1917
Miscellaneous	D.A.G. 3rd Echelon	01/05/1917	01/05/1917
War Diary	Sailly	01/04/1917	24/04/1917
War Diary	Sailly Sur Lys	30/04/1917	30/04/1917
Heading	War Diary Of "A" & "Q" 57th Division 1st May 1917-31st May 1917 Vol 4		
War Diary	Sailly	01/05/1917	02/05/1917
War Diary	Croix Du Bac	05/05/1917	30/06/1917
Heading	57 Division A & Q		
Heading	War Diary Headquarters, 57th Division "A"and"Q" Vol 6		
Miscellaneous	War Diaries		
War Diary	Croix du Bac.	01/07/1917	27/07/1917
Heading	WO95/2967		
War Diary	Croix du Bac	29/07/1917	17/09/1917
War Diary	Norrent Fontes	20/09/1917	30/09/1917
Heading	Cover for Documents. Nature Of Enclosures. War Diary "A" & "Q" 57 Division October 1917		
War Diary	Norrent Fontes	04/10/1917	17/10/1917
War Diary	Renescure	18/10/1917	18/10/1917
War Diary	Proven	19/10/1917	24/10/1917
War Diary	Welsh Farm	25/10/1917	30/10/1917
Heading	War Diary "A" & "Q" Headquarters, 57th Division. November 1917 Vol 10		
War Diary	Elverdinghe	02/11/1917	08/11/1917
War Diary	Cocove	09/11/1917	09/11/1917
War Diary	Chateau	10/11/1917	10/11/1917
War Diary	Nr Andrieq	11/11/1917	13/11/1917
War Diary	Cocove Chateau	15/11/1917	30/11/1917
War Diary	Cocove Chateau	08/12/1917	08/12/1917
War Diary	Proven	09/12/1917	17/12/1917
War Diary	Elverdinghe Chateau	18/12/1917	30/12/1917
Heading	War Diary 57th Division "A" & "Q" January 1918 Vol 12		

War Diary	Elverdinghe	01/01/1918	03/01/1918
War Diary	Steenwerck	04/01/1918	31/01/1918
War Diary	Steenwerck	05/02/1918	11/02/1918
War Diary	Merville	16/02/1918	28/02/1918
Heading	War Diary Headquarters 57th Division, "A" & "Q" March, 1918 Vol 14		
War Diary	Merville	02/03/1918	14/03/1918
War Diary	Croix Du Bac	21/03/1918	28/03/1918
Heading	Administrative 57th Div. A. & Q. 57th Division April 1918		
Heading	A & "Q" Branch Headquarters 57th Division. Original War Diary April 1918		
War Diary	Croix Du Bac	01/04/1918	01/04/1918
War Diary	Merville	02/04/1918	02/04/1918
War Diary	Lucheux	02/04/1918	03/04/1918
War Diary	Couturelle	05/04/1918	08/04/1918
War Diary	Beauquesne	09/04/1918	09/04/1918
War Diary	Lucheux	12/04/1918	12/04/1918
War Diary	Pas	14/04/1918	30/04/1918
Heading	Original War Diary. May 1918. Vol 16		
War Diary	Pas	01/05/1918	06/05/1918
War Diary	Couin	07/05/1918	31/05/1918
Miscellaneous	57th Division.	01/06/1918	01/06/1918
Miscellaneous	C.R.A., 57th Division	11/05/1918	11/05/1918
Heading	War Diary "A" & "Q" 57 Div. Vol 17		
War Diary	Couin	01/06/1918	02/07/1918
War Diary	Authie	04/07/1918	15/07/1918
War Diary	Pas	16/07/1918	29/07/1918
War Diary	Bouquemaison	30/07/1918	30/07/1918
Heading	Original War Diary "A" & "Q" Branch 57th Division August 1918 Vol 19		
War Diary	Hermaville	02/08/1918	02/08/1918
War Diary	Etrun	02/08/1918	18/08/1918
War Diary	Chelers	19/08/1918	22/08/1918
War Diary	Rebreuve	28/08/1918	28/08/1918
War Diary	Bavincourt	24/08/1918	27/08/1918
War Diary	Mercatel	27/08/1918	31/08/1918
Heading	Original War Diary. September, 1918 57th Division "A" & "Q" Branch. Vol 20		
War Diary	Blairville	03/09/1918	12/09/1918
War Diary	Queant	14/09/1918	17/09/1918
War Diary	Bavincourt	18/09/1918	26/09/1918
War Diary	Queant	27/09/1918	28/09/1918
War Diary	Nr Pronville	30/09/1918	30/09/1918
Heading	Original War Diary October "A" & "Q" 57 Division Vol 21		
War Diary	Near Cambai	03/10/1918	11/10/1918
War Diary	Barlin	12/10/1918	12/10/1918
War Diary	Epinette	14/10/1918	14/10/1918
War Diary	Fromelles	17/10/1918	18/10/1918
War Diary	Ronchin	19/10/1918	20/10/1918
War Diary	Willems	31/10/1918	31/10/1918
War Diary	Mons-En Baroeul	01/11/1918	30/11/1918
War Diary	Mons-En-Baroeuil	02/12/1918	02/12/1918
War Diary	Duisans	06/12/1918	25/06/1919

WO 95/2967/2

57 DIVISION
HQ BRANCHES / SERVICES
ADJUTANT / QM GENERAL
Feb 1917 - June 1919

57TH DIVISION

'A' & 'Q' BRANCH FEB 1917 - JUN 1919

1917 FEB — 1919 JUN

WAR DIARY
~~INTELLIGENCE SUMMARY~~

(Erase heading not required.)

Army Form C. 2118.

Place	Date	Hour	Summary of Events and Information	Remarks and references to Appendices
Boulogne	2.2.17	—	G.S.O 2 (Major H.G.A Thomson) D.A.A + Q.M.G (Major B.S Moss-Blundell) Staff Captains of R.A. 170th 171st 172nd Bdes arrived.	AMS
Bailleul	3.2.17		G.S.O 2. D.A.A + Q.M.G reported to Hq. II Anzac Corps and received orders re. concentrating areas and advance tactical parties.	AMS
Sailly Sur Lys	4.2.17		Advance tactical parties 82 Officers and 200 O.R arrived and were attached to R.A. R.E. and Infantry of New Zealand Division for instruction.	AMS
	5.2.17 to 9.2.17		D.A.A + Q.M.G and Staff Captains engaged in allotting billeting areas. R.A. Hq. at Neuf Berquin 170th Outtersteen 171st Bde at Strazeele. 172nd Bde at Borre all in the Merris area.	AMS
	10.2.17		Arrivals in concentration area 285th Bde R.F.A. 1 Regnt and medium 2/5 K.O. R. Lancs Regt.	AMS
	11.2.17		Arrivals in concentration area A Bats. 287th Bde R.F.A. 2/4 L.N Lancs Regt.	AMS
	12.2.17		Arrivals in concentration area D Bats. 286th Bde R.F.A and remainder 287th Bde.	AMS
	13.2.17		Arrivals A + C Bats. 286th Bde R.F.A. 2/5 L.N Lancs Regt. 2/5 K.O.R Lancs Regt and 2/4 L.N Lancs Regt moved into the line and took over from 3rd New Zealand Infantry Brigade. Also 285 Bde R.F.A completed line.	AMS

73

Army Form C. 2118.

WAR DIARY
or
~~INTELLIGENCE SUMMARY.~~
(Erase heading not required.)

Instructions regarding War Diaries and Intelligence Summaries are contained in F. S. Regs., Part II. and the Staff Manual respectively. Title pages will be prepared in manuscript.

74

Place	Date	Hour	Summary of Events and Information	Remarks and references to Appendices
Merris Area	14·2·17		Arrivals in concentration area. 170th Light T.M.B. 505 Coy. A.S.C. 2/2 West Lancs Field Amb. C Batty 286th Bde. C.R.E. and 1/3 West Lancs Field Coy R.E.	A3
"	15·2·17		Arrivals. 57th Div. Sig. Coy. 170th Bde Hq. 4/5 Loyal North Lancs. 170th M.G.C. 506 Coy A.S.C. Saw Section Divisional Headquarters. Lt-Col W.M.S. Stewart A.D.M.S. D'A.D.M.S. A.P.M. Camp Cmdt. A.D.V.S.	A3
"	16·2·17		Arrivals in concentration area. No 1 Sec. D.A.C. 2/2 Wessex Field Coy. R.E. 171st Bde Hq. 2/5 + 2/6 King's Liverpool Regts. 171st L.T.M.B. 171st M.G.C. 507 A.S.C. 2/3 Wessex Field Amb. A+Q offices Div Hq. Formed. No Q staff present with Div.	A3
Bailleul	17·2·17		Q.O.C and Q S.O. arrived and stayed night with Corps Cmdr.	A3
Merris Area	17·2·17		Arrivals in concentration area. No 2 Sec D.A.C. 2/3 Wessex Field Coy R.E. 2/7 + 2/8 King's Liverpool Regt. 2/2 Wessex field Amb.	A3
"	18·2·17		Arrivals in concentration area. 3rd Q. 172nd Bde. 2/4 S. Lancs Regt. 172nd M.G.C. 172nd L.T.M.B. 508 A.S.C. Q got arrived at Div. Hq. 170th Bde. Opened took over night sector of line from 3rd N.Z. Bde. Headquarters of Bde at Rouge du Bout	A3
Sailly				

Army Form C. 2118.

WAR DIARY
or
INTELLIGENCE SUMMARY

(Erase heading not required.)

Instructions regarding War Diaries and Intelligence Summaries are contained in F. S. Regs., Part II. and the Staff Manual respectively. Title pages will be prepared in manuscript.

Place	Date	Hour	Summary of Events and Information	Remarks and references to Appendices
Merris Area	18/2/17		Arrived in concentration Area No 3 Section D.A.C.	
Sailly	20.2.17		171st Bde opened move from Strazeele to Sailly & Estaires area.	PMO
"	21.2.17		" commenced relief of 1st New Zealand Bde in Bonttillerie section. Arrived in concentration area. 2/5 South Lancs Regt.	PMO
Merris				PMO
Sailly	22.2.17		171st Bde completed relief of 1st NZ Bde.	PMO
"	23.2.17		Arrived in concentration area 2/10 Liverpools. 172nd Bde opened movement taking over Bois Grenier sub-section from 2nd & 2. Bde. Orders received for trekking up 287th Bde R.F.A. A battery (18 pdrs) to go to 175th Army Field Arty Bde. B Batt (18 pdrs) to 3rd Army. Right section C Batty (4.5") to 66th Div. Left sect C. Batty to 59th Div. Each keep their batteries & D.A.C. to make up Bde Amm Column. No 3 Sect. to be broken up. D.A.Q informed for England.	PMO
Merris	2.4.3.17		Div Hq without command of army troops except headquarters.	PMO
Sailly	25.3.17 12 nn		Div Hq opened at Sailly and took over command of night Sect II Army Corps MO. Total casualties for month Officers, 1 missing, 1 wounded. O.R. 17 killed, 1 missing, 35 wounded, 4 self inflicted, 123 sick	PMO

Approved report
Lt General
cmdg 57th Divn

15 US

WAR DIARY
or
INTELLIGENCE SUMMARY.
(Erase heading not required.)

Army Form C. 2118.

HQ A 5 172 Vol II

Place	Date	Hour	Summary of Events and Information	Remarks and references to Appendices
Saills	6.3.17		Orders received for Bde to be considerably increased and to be held by 2 Bdes with one Bde in Divisional Reserve.	A3
"	14.3.17		2nd Lt. Humphreys took over as DADOS vice Capt Burgham	A
"	16.3.17		Capt Duke DAQMG referred rich with measles. The latter disease attached several other officers about that time.	
"			35 Officers arrived as reinforcements.	A3
"	28.3.17		Major St. G. A. Thomson OBO2 died of wounds rec'd by shell near La Vesse	A3
"	29.3.17		Buried at Saills Sur lys by Senr. Chaplains conducted service, all divisional staff present + also officers from each Bde Hy.	
"			Reinforcements as follows arrived 2/5 KOLR 6 4 OR. 2/4 L.F. 45 OR. 2/5 L.F.2 4 8 OR. 4/5 L.F. 29 L.F. 46 OR.	
"			8 Officers wounded accidentally by explosion at Bombing lecture 170th Bde.	A3
"	31.3.17		Lt-Col G.W.S. Sharpe 2/5 K O Lanc Regt left for England on vacating command.	
			Total casualties for month. Officers Killed 1. Wounded 23. Sick 37.	
			Other Ranks killed 33. missing 2. wounded 188. sick 1217. self inflicted 7.	A0

E J Brackenbury Lieut-General
Cmd. 57th Division

D.A.G.
3rd Echelon

57th (W. LANCS.) DIVISION
CONFIDENTIAL
No. C 68
Date 1/5/17

Herewith War Diary in duplicate for month of April 1917 for A+Q Branch 57th Division.

1/5/17.

R.W.R. Barnes Major
Lieut. General
Cmdg 57th Division.

① April 1917.

57TH (W. LANCS.) DIVISION
CONFIDENTIAL
No. C 68
Date 1/5/17

Vol 3

Army Form C. 2118.

WAR DIARY
or
~~INTELLIGENCE SUMMARY.~~
(Erase heading not required.)

Instructions regarding War Diaries and Intelligence Summaries are contained in F. S. Regs., Part II. and the Staff Manual respectively. Title pages will be prepared in manuscript.

Place	Date	Hour	Summary of Events and Information	Remarks and references to Appendices
Sailly	1.4.17		Lt. Col. W. Simpson 286th Bde R.F.A proceeded to England on vacation command & is rel[ieve]d by Lt. Col. R.C. Davis	143.
	2.4.17		Major Derry DSO Welsh Regt Bde Major Bde joined as GSO2 to Div	140
	6.4.17		Bdr. Gen. H.R. Brown DSO took over command of 171st Bde vice Bdr-General A R Gillett DSO.	140
	7.4.17		Bdr-General A R Gillett DSO left for England	140
	7.4.17		Major H. P. Creagh Osborn 1st Royal Lancaster Regt arrived & reptd for instruction	140
	8.4.17		" " " took over temp. command of 2/5th B. Lancs Rgt	140
	9.4.17		Major G. A. Ballard 1st Oxford and Bucks L.I. took over temp command of 2/4 O.B. Regt	140
	12.4.17		Draft of 23 O.R. joined 2/10 K.L.R. Lt-Col Faine 2/10 K.L.R. & Lt-Col D. Bates 2/5	140
	10.4.17		left for England. Major E. G. Rabbiski took over command of 2/10 KLR	140
	15.4.17		Capt. QM Birkett staff Capt 172nd Bde appointed D.A.A.G 2nd Div[ision]	140
	18.4.17		Draft of 62 O.R. arrived for 2/10 K. Liverpools	140
	20.4.17		Lt-Col Short arrived to take command of 286th Bde R.F.A.	140
	21.4.17		Major E.L. Andrews a/c South Cheshire Regt joined 172nd Bde pending posting to command 2/5 South Lancs	140
	24.4.17		15 officers arrived as reinforcements for 171st Bde. Lieut H.R. Hennelly M.C. Royal Fusiliers appointed Intelligence Off Staff Capt[ain] 172nd (Brigade)	140

① April 1917.

Army Form C. 2118.

WAR DIARY
or
INTELLIGENCE SUMMARY.

57TH (W. LANCS.) DIVISION
CONFIDENTIAL
No. C 68
Date 1/5/17

Place	Date	Hour	Summary of Events and Information	Remarks and references to Appendices
Saillis	1/4/17		Lt-Col W. Simpson 286th Bde RFA proceeded to England on vacation command & is succeeded by Lt-Col R.C. Drury	143
	2/4/17		Major Devitt DSO Welsh Regt Bde Major joined as Staff Off 2 to Div.	143
	6/4/17		Bdr-Gen H.K. Bray DSO took over command of 171st Bde vice Bde General A.R. Gillett DSO	143
	7/4/17		Bdr-General A.R. Gillett DSO left for England	143
	7/4/17		Major H.P. Creagh Osborne 1st Royal Lancaster Regt arrived & reported for instruction	143
	8/4/17		" " took over temp. command of 2/5 K.B. Lancs Rgt	143
	9/4/17		Major J.A. Ballard 1st Oxfd & Bucks L.I. took over temp command of 2/10 K.B. Regt.	143
	12/4/17		Draft of 230 O.R joined 2/10 K.L.R; Lt-Col Fawne 2/10 K.L.R & Lt-Col D Balbo 2/5 Cheshire Rgt	143
	15/4/17		" " Major E.L. Robertson took over command of 2/10 K.L.R left for England.	143
	18/4/17		Capt GH Birkett Adjt Capt 172nd Bde attached DAAG 3rd Dunme	143
	20/4/17		Draft of 62 O.R arrived for 2/10 K. Rinforce	143
	21/4/17		Lt-Col Short arrived to take command of 286th Bde RFA.	143
	24/4/17		Major E.L. Ambrose of South Cheshire Regt joined 172nd Bde pending posting to command 2/5 South Lancs	143
			15 officers arrived as reinforcements for 171st Bde Lieut H.H. Hennessey M.C. Regd Fusilrs assumed duties as	143

② April 1917.

WAR DIARY
or
INTELLIGENCE SUMMARY.
(Erase heading not required.)

Army Form C. 2118.

Place	Date	Hour	Summary of Events and Information	Remarks and references to Appendices
Saillie au Bac	30.4.17		Draft of 3 officers for 170th Bde and 1 for 171st Bde arrived.	MS
	30.4.17		Officers serving on Divisional Staff at end of month. G.O.C. Lt. Gen. R.G. Broadwood C.B.	
			A.D.C.'s Capt. Y.B. Jammens (Cnds Gnds) Cheshire Regt. Lieut. H.W. Fletcher Lanc. Hussars.	
			G.S.O.1. Lieut. Col. C.Y.L. Allanson C.I.E. D.S.O. G.S.O.2 Major A. Denny 3rd Welsh Regt.	
			G.S.O.3 Capt. R.G. Agar Rifle Bde. (S.R.)	
			A.A.+Q.M.G Lt.Col. W.M. Stewart Camerons Highlanders	
			D.A.A.G. Major B. Shaw-Blundell 3rd/4th Gordon Highrs D.A.Q.M.G Capt. A.C.H. Duke R.F.O.	
			A.D.M.S. Colonel A.F. Dewar A.M.S. DADMS Capt J.F. Edmiston RAMC(T)	
			ADVS Major P.W. Dargh Smith A.V.C. A.P.M. Major W. Blaquere 6th Royal	
			Scots Fusiliers. Senior Chaplain Rev Canon St.m. L.F. Tognchitt 3rd Y.O.C.F.	
			DADOS. Lieut. B.L. Humphreys. A.O.C.	MS
			Total Casualties for month Officers Killed 2 wounded 17. missing 3. sick 22	
			Other Ranks Killed 44. wounded 263. missing 7. Sick 944. Self inflicted. 4.	
			5 cases tried. Pet.	

R.G. Broadwood Lieut-General
Cmdg 57th Division.

② April 1917

Army Form C. 2118.

WAR DIARY
or
INTELLIGENCE SUMMARY.
(Erase heading not required.)

Place	Date	Hour	Summary of Events and Information	Remarks and references to Appendices
Saulty and dues	30.4.17		Draft of 3 officers for 170th Bde and 1 for 171st Bde arrived.	mis
	30.4.17		Officers serving as Divisional Staff at end of month.	
			G.O.C. Lt-Gen R.G. Broadwood	
			A.D.C.'s Capt S.B. Garmany (Intelth) Chelsea Yeo. Lieut H.H. Fletcher Lancs Hussars	
			G.S.O.1. Lieut.Col C.J.L. Allanson C.I.E D.S.O	
			G.S.O.2 Major A. Denny DSO Welsh Regt.	
			G.S.O.3 Capt R.G. Glyn Rifle Bde (S.R.)	
			A.A.+Q.M.G Lt-Col W.H. Stewart Cameron Highlanders	
			D.A.A.G. Major B.S.Thos-Blunden DSO (intch Rifle Bde)	
			D.A.Q.M.G Capt A.C.H Duke R.F.O.	
			A.D.M.S. Colonel A.F.Dennar A.M.S. DADMS Capt J.F.Edmiston RAMC (T)	
			A.D.V.S Major P.W Dargue Smith A.V.C. A.P.M. Major W. Blayney 6th Royal Irish Fusiliers Senior Chaplain Rev Canon Hon L.F. Tapwhite Jn V.O. C.F.	
			D.A.D.O.S. Lieut. C.L. Humphrey A.O.C.	M3
			Total Casualties for month Officers Killed 2 wounded 17 missing 3 Sick 22. Other Ranks Killed 44, wounded 263, missing 7. Sick 944 Self inflicted 4. 5 cases trench feet.	

M.G.Broadwood Lieut-General
Comdg 57th Division.

Vol 4

Confidential
War Diary
of
"A" & "Q" Branch
57th Division

1st May 1917 – 31st May 1917

Army Form C. 2118.

WAR DIARY
or
INTELLIGENCE SUMMARY. 57th. Division A + Q Branch
(Erase heading not required.)

Place	Date	Hour	Summary of Events and Information	Remarks and references to Appendices
Sailly	17/3/17		Draft of 13 OR arrived for Div Arty	1963
	2/5/17		Headquarters of Division arrived & Croix du Bac + took over H.Q. of 3rd Australian Division	900
Croix du Bac	5/5/17		Draft of 64 OR for 2/4 South Lancs Regt arrived. Lt Col R.S. Dunn left & ordered Dep of Brigade. Draft of 40 OR for Div Arty arrived	1963
	9/5/17		Bdr Gen a. Martin proceeded home on going up command of 17th Brigade. Draft of 40 OR for Div Arty arrived	900
Croix du Bac	10/5/17		Bdr Gen F.G. Aynesting CMG took over command of 170th Bde. Draft of 27 OR arrived for 2/10 Loyal'l Regt.	900
"	10/5/17		Temp Major (Capt.) W. L. Owen M.C. 5th Princ'pals took over command of 2/5 South Lancs.	900
	15/5/17		Draft of 10 OR for 2/10 Loyal'l Regt arrived	1963
	18/5/17		Lt Gen Plumer G.C.M.G. K.C.M.G. cmdg 2nd Army presented military medals to N.C.Os + men of the Division	900
"	19/5/17		Draft of 41 OR arrived for 4/5 Loyal North Lancs. Regt.	900
"	20/5/17		Division transferred to XI Corps 1st Army from II Anzac Corps 2nd Army	900
"	24/5/17		GOC Division proceeded on 10 days leave to England.	1963
"	24/5/17		2 Coys 49th Division attached to Division.	900
"	25/5/17		Lt + Qmr S Burbank 2/5 Loyal North Lancs Regt proceeded to England.	1963

Army Form C. 2118.

WAR DIARY
or
INTELLIGENCE SUMMARY.
(Erase heading not required.)

A. & Q. Branch 57th Divn

Place	Date	Hour	Summary of Events and Information	Remarks and references to Appendices
Croix du Bac	29/5/17		Lt. & Qmr A.E. Bolton 2/8 Liverpool Regt. arrived	AQ3
	31/5/17		General Court Martial held on Lt. J.H. Glancey 2/8 Kings Liverpool Regt.	AQ3
	31/5/17		Divisional Staff at end of month. G.O.C. Bdr-Genl J.C. Wray C.M.G. M.V.O. vice Bt-General R.G. Broadwood C.B. (as killed). GSO1 Lt-Col C.J.L. Allanson C.I.E. D.S.O. GSO II (a) Major Denny D.S.O. GSO III Capt R.G. Ogilvie A.A. & Q.M.G. Lt-Col W.Gn. Stewart D.A.Q.G Major B.S. Innes-Blundell D.S.O. S.A.S.H.G Captain R.C.H. Duke A.D.M.S. Colonel F.W. Dewar D.D.M.S. Capt J.F. Edmondson D.A.D.O.S. Lt.B.A. Humphreys A.D.V.S. Major Danger-Smith A.R.N. Major P. Blampin A.D.C. Capt R.P. J'annoens and Lt H.F. Fletcher Senior Chapl. Rev. Carnes F. Typewriter W. No	
			Total casualties for month := Officers. Killed 1. Wounded 27. Sick 42. Other Ranks. Killed 64 Wounded 355. Missing 16. Sick 973. Self inflicted 9.	AQ3

Signed
Lt Bdr General
Comdg 57th Divn.

Army Form C. 2118.

57th (W. Lancs.) Division
SECRET S68
Intelligence 30/6/17

WAR DIARY
or
INTELLIGENCE SUMMARY.   A + Q. Branch 57th Division
(Erase heading not required.)

Place	Date	Hour	Summary of Events and Information	Remarks and references to Appendices
Croix du Bac.	2.6.17		2/4 Loyal North Lancs + 2/5 Loyal North Lancs. attached to 3rd Australian Div. under Major Geddes Bde Major 171st Bde for Battle of Messines. They suffered 190 Casualties. This place in 170th Bde. was taken by 1/4 + 1/5 West Riding Regt.	A13.
	11.6.17		Capt. R.A.R. Van Agnisen 2/9 North R Regt. despatched to England.	A13
	11.6.17		Capt. C.L. Fox assumed cmd. 502 Coy. R.E. vice W. Jane evacuated to England 1/6/17	A13
	14.6.17		R.Q.M. Sergt H.H. Ball 2/9 North R Regt appointed Quartermaster of Bw	A13.
	17.6.17		Lt. Col. H.D. Booth 2/3 Wessex F.A. attached A.D.M.S. 55th Division	A13
	18.6.17		Divisional Horse Show held at Nouveau Monde. A great success. Lt.-Gen. Plumer D.C.M.G. & K.C.M.G. attended. A heavy thunderstorm broke over the ground	A13
	" "		in the afternoon.	
	21.6.17		Lt-General R.O. Broadwood CB. Gpl. 57th Division died of wounds received while He was struck by a shell while crossing the railway bridge over the River Lys at Houplines at 10.15 am. He died in the 54th Casualty Clearing Station at Estaires. Lt- Col W.A. Stark C.M.G. cmdg 28th Bde R.F.A. who was with him was also killed.	A13.
	22.6.17		Funeral of Gen. Broadwood at Sailly sur Lys. Very large attendence includen Lt. Gen. Sir H.S. Horne K.C.B. cmdr. 1st Army and many officers & 12 Lancers. The Generals P.d. Regt. Pipe	

WAR DIARY or INTELLIGENCE SUMMARY

Army Form C. 2118.

A. & Q. Branch 57th Division.

Place	Date	Hour	Summary of Events and Information	Remarks and references to Appendices
Croix du Bac.	25.6.17		Captain S.T. Lucey M.C. B.de-Major 172nd Bde. appointed O/B O.II. 66th Divn. and left same day.	A.O
	" " "		Lt. Col. E.W. Shedding assumed cmd. 286th Bde.	A.O
	" " "		Capt. A.M. Bellingham 173rd M. of Cos. appointed Div. M.G. Officer	A.O
	29.6.17		Captain J.L. Alexander London Regt. joined as Acting B.de Major 171st Bde.	A.O
	30.6.17		Major Geddes D.S.O. B.de Major 171st left to take up appointment as O/B O.II 8th Divn. Capt. W.H. Maxwell A.D.C. to new B.OC arrived.	A.O
	25.6.17		Major (Temp.Lt.Col.) J. Nightingale R.A.M.C. T.F. assumed command of 2/3 Wessex F.A.	A.O
	2.6.17		Inclus. of 248th Employment Coy 1 Off. 105 O.R. arrived	A.O
	30.6.17		Divisional Staff. B.de Gen J. C. Wray CMG. M.V.O. Q.St. A.D.C² Lieut H. M. Fletcher. Capt. I.B. Jamous. Gen Staff. Lt.Col. Allanson C.I.E. D.S.O. Major A. Denny D.S.O. Capt. R.g.C. Ofip. A&Q.branch. Lt.Col. W.Mr. S.Stewart. Major B.S. Moor Blundell D.S.O. Capt. A.C.H.Duke. A.D.M.S. Col. T.F. Dewar. D.A.D M.S. Capt. J.F. Edmunds. A.D.V.S. Major P. Dauge-Smith. D.A.D.O.S. Lieut. B.L. Humphreys. A.P.M. Major W. Blayney.
			Total Casualties from mdt. Offs. K.6. W.36. M.3. Sich 33. Other Ranks: K.89. W. 614. M.41 Sich 825. Self Inf. W.14	M.B. Rowland from B.de Gen. Cmd. 57th Divn.

57 DIVISION

A & Q

Box 2967

1 ENTRY

WO 154/71

WAR DIARY.

JULY.

Headquarters, 57th Division.

"A" and "Q".

War Diaries

① Original Removed to
W/O 154/71

57th (W. Lancs.) Division

SECRET
No. S68.
Date 1.8.17 A+Q Branch 57th Division

Army Form C. 2118.

WAR DIARY
or
INTELLIGENCE SUMMARY.
(Erase heading not required.)

Instructions regarding War Diaries and Intelligence
Summaries are contained in F. S. Regs., Part II.
and the Staff Manual respectively. Title pages
will be prepared in manuscript.

Place	Date	Hour	Summary of Events and Information	Remarks and references to Appendices
Croix du Bac.	1-7-17		Major-General R.W.R. Barnes C.B. D.S.O. (h.p) assumed command of Division	A3
"			Capt. W. St. G. Clones R.f.O. 19th Hussars ADC to GOC arrived	A3
"	4-7-17		Capt. C. J. Gasson M.C. South Lancashire Regt. took over command of 2/4 Loyal North Lanc. Regt. vice Lt-Col Ballard (to England)	A3
"	9-7-17		Capt. W.H.S. Alston M.C. took over duties of Bde Major 172nd Bde.	A3
"	8-7-17		Draft of 67 OR 2/5 Loyal North Lancs. arrived for 2/7 K.L. Regt.	A3
"	10-7-17		" 37 OR arrived for 2/6 K.L. Regt.	A3
"	10-7-17		" "	A3
"	10-7-17		" 67 OR arrived for 2/5 Loyal North Lancs	A3
"	18-7-17			A3
"	14-7-17		16 Companies of 4th Bde C.E. Rotingen attached to Brigade at a time for period of 4 days	A3
"	29-7-17		Lt-Col (Maj) J.R. Welland DSO Gloucester Regt affointed and arrived duties GSO1 to Division vice T. Lieut-Col (Major) C.L. Allanson CIE	A3
"	27-7-17		DSO who departed to England for duty in India	A3

w/o 95/2967

Q + Q Branch
Army Form C. 2118.

57th Division.

WAR DIARY

(Erase heading not required.)

Place	Date	Hour	Summary of Events and Information	Remarks and references to Appendices
Croix du Bac	29/7/17 30/7/17		Armentières very heavily shelled by mustard oil & gas shells during night of 29/30. There were 954 cases of gas chiefly in the 2/5 & 2/6 Kings Liverpool Regiment. Both Bns. but the C.Os. who were slightly gassed.	A/3
"	31/7/17		1st Leicestershire and 4th Norfolk Regts attached to Division during change of 171st Bde. not from Armentières to Fleurbaix sector with 170th Bde.	A/3
"			Division Staff. GSO1 Major-Genl. R.W.R. Barnes CB DSO. ADC Capt W. St Q. Clarere. ADC. C.C. Capt W.O. Manwell. GSO1. Major (T.Lt.Col) S R Wetherd DSO. GSO II. Major. C.J.P. RBG. GSO III DAQMG Lt.Col W. Sn. Stewart DAAQ Mar. B.S. Grun-Blundell DSO. DAQMG Capt. A.C.H. Duke. ADMS Col C.T.F. Trevor. DADMS. Capt. J. F. Edmiston. DADS Lieut. C. J. Humphrys. APM Major W. Braxmus. Senior Chaplain Canon Stn. L. Trumbull M.D. Casualties during the month. Officers killed 2. wounded 84 missing 1 Sick 20. Other Ranks Killed 103. wounded 1752. missing 12. Sick 799. Self inflicted 7.	

R.M. Blundell Major
DAAQ
t. Major General Commanding
57th Division

HQ AQ 5-7D
Army Form C. 2118

Vol 7

WAR DIARY
or
INTELLIGENCE SUMMARY
(Erase heading not required.)

Instructions regarding War Diaries and Intelligence Summaries are contained in F. S. Regs., Part II. and the Staff Manual respectively. Title pages will be prepared in manuscript.

Place	Date	Hour	Summary of Events and Information	Remarks and references to Appendices
Croix du Bac.	1.8.17		Major A. Dennis departed to take up position of ADMS II X14 Corps	A53.
"	4.8.17		Capt. P.H. Hansen V.C. M.C. arrived duty as ADMS II Division.	A53.
"	5.8.17		Major E.V. Manager 2nd Durham Light Infantry assumed command of 2/9 Kings Liverpool Regiment.	A0
"	5.8.17		Capt. G.L. Alexander M.C. London Regt. Bde Major 171st Bde killed re Bomb from Bosch Aeroplane.	A0
"	9.8.17		Lt. R.W. Patteson M.C. Suffolk Regt. assumed duties as Bde Major 171st Bde.	A0
"	16.8.17		Capt. W.J. Jarvis M.C. Inniskillen Regt. assumed duties as Bde Major 170th Bde	A0
"	13.8.17		Draft of 119 OR arrived for 2/6 K.L. Regt.	A0
"	13.8.17		Major M.J.G. Jenkins Service Regt. arrived command of 2/5 K.L. Regt.	A0
"	13.8.17		Capt. R.A.C. Flynn ADMS posted to Egypt forwarded to England but found medically unfit for service in Egypt + returned on 30/8/17 to duty as ADMS	A53.

WAR DIARY
or
INTELLIGENCE SUMMARY.
(Erase heading not required.)

Army Form C. 2118.

Place	Date	Hour	Summary of Events and Information	Remarks and references to Appendices
Croydon Bar	16.8.17		Draft of 103 OR for 2/5 K.L. Regt. 248 OR for 2/6 K.L.R.	AO
"	17.8.17		Draft of 129 OR for 2/7 K.L.R.	AO
"	19.8.17		Draft of 61 OR for 2/8 K.L.R.	AO
"	20.8.17		Lt Col Moss R.F.A attached to R.A pending vacancy for Brigade	AO
"	22.8.17		Draft of 49 OR for D.A.C	AO
"	23.8.17		Draft of 72 OR for 2/10 K.L.R	AO
"	24.8.17		" of 40 OR for 2/8 KLR and 82 OR for 2/6 KLR	AO
"	26.8.17		" 51 OR for 2/5 K.L.R. 36 OR for K.O. Lanc Rgt 45 OR for 2/6 KLR	AO
"			24 for 2/7 KLR.	AO
"	28.8.17		Draft of 23 OR for 2/10 K.L.R	AO
"	29.8.17		" 61 OR for 2/4 L.N. Lanc Rgt and 35 OR for 2/5 L.N. Lancs Rgt	AO
"			Divisional Boxing Tournament held at Bar St Maur Opened_ men and were largely attended by all ranks.	AO
"	30.8.17		Draft of 25 OR for D.A.C. 101 OR for 2/4 South Lancs Regt	AO
"	31.8.17		Divisional Staff at end of month Gen Major- Gen R W R Bgnes CB	AB
			DSO ADC Capt Sr G Clerke Capt W B Maxwell (Coldm Gnds)	AB

WAR DIARY
~~INTELLIGENCE SUMMARY~~
(Erase heading not required.)

Army Form C. 2118.

Place	Date	Hour	Summary of Events and Information	Remarks and references to Appendices
Croix du Bac	31/8/17		1917 Lt-Col. J.R. Wethered D.S.O. G.S.O.ⁱ Capt. P.R. Hawers V.C. M.C. G.S.O.ⁱⁱ Capt R.O.E. Glynn. A.A.Q.M.G. Lt.Col. W.M. Stewart. D.A.A.G. Major B.S.M. Blundell D.S.O. D.A.Q.M.G. Major A.C.H. Duke A.D.M.S. Col. T.F. Devine. D.A.D.M.S. Capt. J.F. Edmistor. D.A.D.V.S Major P.W. Dauger-Smith. D.A.D.O.S. Lieut. B.L. Humphreys. a/D.D. Major W. Blampur. Senior Chaplain Canon Hon. Lt. Tyrwhitt M.O.	
	31/8/17		Casualties for month Officers Killed 2. wounded 7. missing 2. sick 15 Other ranks. Killed 68. wounded 449. Self inflicted 2. missing 9. sick 241	

M.M.Blundell Major
for
Major-General
Cmdg. 5th Division.

Sept 1917
Army Form C. 2118

67th (W. Lancs.) Division
SECRET
MA 0905

WAR DIARY
or
INTELLIGENCE SUMMARY.
(Erase heading not required.)

Instructions regarding War Diaries and Intelligence Summaries are contained in F. S. Regs., Part II. and the Staff Manual respectively. Title pages will be prepared in manuscript.

Place	Date	Hour	Summary of Events and Information	Remarks and references to Appendices
Croix du Bac	2.9.17		Major (2nd Lt) R.S.H. Stafford assumed command of 2/7 K.L.R.	FB.
"	10.9.17		Capt (T. Major) C.S. Barnes DSO Oxford & Bucks L.I. assumed command of 2/7 KLR vice Major Stafford posted to command of Middlesex Regt.	MS.
"	12.9.17		Lt-Qmr T.R. Sillem joined 2/6 K.L.R.	MS.
"	15.9.17		Lieut-Col E.B. Cotter assumed command of 228th Bde. vice Lt-Col E.B. Sheddon who joined 3rd Division.	MS.
"	17.9.17		Divnl Headquarters moved to NORRENT FONTES leaving relieved by 38th Division & Artillery who remained in line.	MS.
Norrent Fontes	20.9.17		Drafts for R.F.A. 36 O.R. 25 K.L.R. 130 O.R. 2/6 K.L.R. 130 O.R. 2/7 K.L.R. 130 O.R. 2/7 K.L.R. 130 O.R. 2/8 K.L.R. 88 O.R. 2/7 K.L.R. Major J.S. Cameron 25th Royal Fusiliers assumed command 2/5 KOLR vice	MS.
"	"		Lt.Col Creagh Osborne posted to Adjutant Sr. Officers School	MS.
"	21.9.17		Bde. Gen. R.J. Bruce DSO reverts regimental to take his leave	MS.
"	22.9.17		Lt.Col F.C. Longbourne 2nd West Surrey Regt. assumed command of 171st Bde.	MS.
"	23.9.17		Drafts for 2/5 K.L.R. 50 O.R. 2/7 K.L.R. 50 O.R. 2/8 K.L.R. 50 O.R. 2/9 K.L.R. 37 O.R.	MS.
"	24.9.17		Drafts for 2/5.KORL 147 O.R. 2/6 L.N.L.R. 80 O.R. 2/5 L.N.L.R. 127 O.R.	MS.
"	25/9/17		Drafts for 2/4 S.L.R. 118 O.R. 2/5 S.L.R. 140 O.R. 2/5 KORL 46 O.R.	

SEPT. 1917.
Army Form C. 2118.

WAR DIARY
or
INTELLIGENCE SUMMARY
(Erase heading not required.)

Place	Date	Hour	Summary of Events and Information	Remarks and references to Appendices
NORRENT	25/9/17		R.C. Chaplain T. Doherty deputed for the 9th Division	
FORTES.	27/9/17		Draft for 2/6 K.L.R. 220 O.R.	
	29/9/17		Draft for R.F.A. 33 O.R.	
	30/9/17		Major A. Bruno 2/5 South Lancashire Regiment left for England.	
	30/9/17		Divisional Staff at the end of the Month. Nil. Same as last month.	
			Casualties for the month :- Officers killed 2. Wounded 7. Missing Nil. Sick 23. O.R. killed 27. Wounded 165. Self inflicted Nil. Missing 6. Sick 654	

Cm Thompson
Major
D.A.A.G. for Brigr General
A.A. & Q.M.G. 57th DIVISION

35807. W16879/M1879 500,000 3/17 R.T. (1074) Forms/W3091/3   Army Form W.3091.

Cover for Documents.

Nature of Enclosures.

Original

War Diary

"A" & "Q"

57" Division

October 1917

Notes, or Letters written.

October 1917.
Army Form C. 2118.

WAR DIARY
or
INTELLIGENCE SUMMARY.
(Erase heading not required.)

Place	Date	Hour	Summary of Events and Information	Remarks and references to Appendices
NORRENT FONTES	4.10.17		Reorganisation of D.A.C. Surplus Personnel: 1 Sergeant, 3 Artificers & 82 Other Ranks - Returned to Base	MO
	7.10.17		Reinforcements 2/8 K.L.R. 50 Other Ranks; 2/7 K.L.R. 26 Other Ranks	MO
	11.10.17		Reinforcements 2/5 K.L.R. 28 Other Ranks	MO
	12.10.17		Reinforcements 4/5 Loyal North Lancs Regt. 28 Other Ranks	MO
	14.10.17		Capt J.F.Edmiston RAMC(T.F) relinquishes appointment of D.A.D.M.S. and is posted to the 2/2 Wessex Field Ambulance	MO
	14.10.17		Capt. M.B. King M.C. reports for duty D.A.D.M.S.	MO
	15.10.17		Reinforcements 2/5 King Own Royal Lancs Regt 29 Other Ranks	MO
	17.10.17		Reinforcements 2/5 King transport Regt 20 Other Ranks; 2/7 King transport Regt 20 Other Ranks	MO
	18.10.17		D.H.Q. move to Renescure	MO
Renescure Proven	19.10.17		D.H.Q. move to Proven	MO
	23.10.17		Reinforcements 2/4 South Lancs Regt. 22 Other Ranks; 2/5 South Lancs Regt. 26 Other Ranks	MO
	28.10.17		Reinforcements 2/4 South Lancs Regt 25 Other Ranks	MO
Webb Farm	25.10.17		D.H.Q. move to Webb Farm	MO
	26.10.17		170th Infy Brigade attached with Polcatpolle Casualties 40 Officers 1124 Other Ranks	MO

October 1917.

Army Form C. 2118.

WAR DIARY
or
INTELLIGENCE SUMMARY.
(Erase heading not required.)

Place	Date	Hour	Summary of Events and Information	Remarks and references to Appendices
Welsh Farm	28/10/17		Reinforcements 2/5 South Lancs Regt 25 Other Ranks	
	30/10/17		Reinforcement 2/10 King Liverpool Regt 50 Other Ranks, 170th M.G. Coy 58 Other Ranks.	
	30/10/17		Major C.E. Bishop Commanding 421 (West Lancs) Field Company R.E.	
			Divisional Staff G.O.C Major General R.W.R. Barnes CB DSO ADC Capt N.S.G. Clinton	
			ADC-CC Capt N.B. Maxwell, GSO1 Major (Temp Lt Col) J.R. Watkins DSO, GSO2 Capt	
			P.H. Hansen V.C M.C GSO3 Capt R.E.C. Glyn, AA & QMG Lt Col W.M. Stewart, DAAG Major	
			B.S.M. Blundell DSO, DAQMG Major A.C.H. Duke, ADMS Col T.E. Dewar DADMS	
			Capt M.S. King M.C. DADVS Major P.W. Dwyer Smith, DADOS Capt R.L. Humphreys, APM	
			Major W. Blayney Senior Chaplain Canon Hon F. Tyrwhitt MVO	
			Missing Nil	
			Casualties for the month :- Officers Killed 15 wounded 46 wounded at duty 2 sick 14	
			OR Killed 252, wounded 1041, wounded at duty 18 Missing 312 Self Inflicted 1 sick 930	

ORIGINAL

W A R   D I A R Y

"A" & "Q"

Headquarters, 57th Division.

****

N O V E M B E R   1917.

Army Form C. 2118.

A. + Q. Branch
57th Divn
NOVEMBER 1917

WAR DIARY
or
INTELLIGENCE SUMMARY.
(Erase heading not required.)

Instructions regarding War Diaries and Intelligence Summaries are contained in F. S. Regs., Part II. and the Staff Manual respectively. Title pages will be prepared in manuscript.

Place	Date	Hour	Summary of Events and Information	Remarks and references to Appendices
Elverdin-	2.11.17		Draft of 22 O.R. for 2/8 K.L.R. and 39 for 2/9 K.L.R. arrived.	A43.
ghe.	3.11.17		" 21 " " R.A.M.C. and 56 for 2/5 Kings Own L.R. arrived.	100
	4.11.17		" " " R.A. and " 41 " " 3.3.O.R. for 2/8 M.	A40
	6.11.17		" 160 " " R.A. and " " " " " for 171st Jn. Q.C.	A40
	8.11.17		" 23 " " 2/4 S.Lanc.R. arrived and 20 for 171st Jn Q.C.	
			Divnal Headquarters moved to Elverdinghe to Cocove Chateau on being withdrawn from the line. During its stay in the line it suffered the following casualties. Officers K.16. W.66. M.2. Other Ranks Killed 315. W. 1766. M. 158. Total 2323.	A43.
Cocove	9.11.17		Draft of 57 O.R. for 2/4 L.F. and 65 O.R. for 2/5 L.F. & 76 O.R. for 4/5 L.F. & 76 for 2/6 K.L.R.	A40
Chateau	10.11.17		" 149 O.R. for R.A. 53 for 2/5 K.L.R. arrived. Rev. P. Coulfield (R.C.) Chaplain arrived.	A43
Nr Audricq	11.11.17		" 22 O.R. for 2/5 K.O.L.R. 40 O.R. for 2/4 Lnd. and 26 for 2/5 Lns.	
			Captain D. C. Hamilton M.C. appointed Asst Staff Captain 165th Bde. official	
			Bde Major 172nd Bde.	
	13.11.17		Capt. P. H. Hames V.C. M.C. appointed G.S.O. II 2nd Anzac Corps and succeeded by	
			Capt. W. H. S. Aldsten M.C. as G.S.O. II 57th Divisn.	
			Draft of 51 O.R. for R.A. arrived.	

No. (2)

Army Form C. 2118.

WAR DIARY
or
INTELLIGENCE SUMMARY.
(Erase heading not required.)

A + Q Branch
57th Div. H.Q. Nov 1917

Place	Date	Hour	Summary of Events and Information	Remarks and references to Appendices
Cocove	15.11.17		Draft of 43 O.R. arrived for R.A.M.C.	A3
Chateau	17.11.17		" 27 O.R. arrived for 2/10 King's Liverpool Regiment.	A3
	23.11.17		Capt. C.V. Fisher-Rowe M.C. Grenadier Guards S.R. attached as Bde. Major 172nd Bde. v.c. Capt. D.C. Hamilton M.C. General List.	A3
	25.11.17		R.F.A. reinforcements 60. O.R.	CO
	26.11.17		Capt. D.C. Hamilton M.C. from Bde Major 172 Bde proceeded to work at XVIII Corps H.Qrs.	CO
	27.11.17		R.F.A. reinforcements 21. O.R.	CO
	28.11.17		2/10 K.L.R. reinforcements 45. O.R.	CO
			Casualties for month of November. Killed. Officers 1. O.R. 42. Wounded officers 11. Other ranks 427. Mentaled duty officers 7. O.R. 19. Missing officers nil. O.R. 1. Rec'd officers CO 18. Other ranks 936. Total officers 38. Other ranks 1425.	CO
	30.11.17		Divisional H.Qr. Staff. G.O.C. Maj Genl. R.W.R. Barnes C.B. H.O. A.A.L. Capt. M. St G. Clowes (R of O) A.D.C. Lieut (Temp Capt) J.B. d'Armay. G.S.O.1 Lt Col J.R. Mellized H.O. G.S.O.2. Capt M.H.S. Holm M.C. G.O.3. Lept. R.G.C. Glyn. APM ... Lyd. M.M. Stewart D.A.A.G. Major B.J. Marr-Blundell K.O. D.A.A.M.G. Major A.C. Hacker – A.D.M.S. Lieut. T.F. Dwyer	CO

Army Form C. 2118.

WAR DIARY
or
INTELLIGENCE SUMMARY.
(Erase heading not required.)

Instructions regarding War Diaries and Intelligence Summaries are contained in F. S. Regs., Part II. and the Staff Manual respectively. Title pages will be prepared in manuscript.

Place	Date	Hour	Summary of Events and Information	Remarks and references to Appendices
			D.A.D.M.S. Captain M.B. King M.C. - D.A.A.H. Major C.N. Mayer-Smith - A.P.M. Major W. Blayney - D.A.Q.M.G. Capt Hon. B.L. Humphreys.	
			Charles Major General for Major General Commdg 57 Div. 1 Dec 1917	

Army Form C. 2118.

A + Q. 57th Divn

WAR DIARY
or
INTELLIGENCE SUMMARY.
(Erase heading not required.)

Instructions regarding War Diaries and Intelligence Summaries are contained in F. S. Regs., Part II. and the Staff Manual respectively. Title pages will be prepared in manuscript.

Place	Date	Hour	Summary of Events and Information	Remarks and references to Appendices
Cocove Chateau	8.12.17		Divisional Headquarters left Cocove for Proven after transfer from the XVIII Corps to the XIX Corps	
Proven	9.12.17		Divisional Headquarters arrived from Proven to Rouckhouse	
	9.12.17		Draft of 10 Other Ranks to 421st Field Coy RE and 20 Other Ranks for 502nd Field Coy RE	
	11.12.17		Draft of 20 Other Ranks for 173rd M.G. Coy	
	13.12.17		Draft 29 Other Ranks for Divisional Employment Coy	
	16.12.17		Major [Lt Col E L Roddy Cheshire Regt] relinquished command of 1st Bat Cheshire Regiment assumed command of 1st Bat Cheshire Regiment. Lt Col W L Brodie V.C. M.C.	
	17.12.17		assumed command of 2/10 K.L.R.	
			Draft of 42 Other Ranks for R.F.A.	
Elverdinghe Chateau	18.12.17		Divisional Headquarters moved to Elverdinghe Chateau	
	18.12.17		Capt J.G. Scriven assumed command of 171st Machine Gun Coy	
	19.12.17		Draft of 11 Other Ranks for 172nd M.G. Coy	
	20.12.17		A/Lt Col (Major) M.G. Jenkins 2/5 K.L.R. wounded and evacuated to C.C.S.	
	23.12.17		Draft of 11 Other Ranks for R.F.A.	

Army Form C. 2118.

WAR DIARY
or
INTELLIGENCE SUMMARY.
(Erase heading not required.)

Place	Date	Hour	Summary of Events and Information	Remarks and references to Appendices
Elverdinghe Chateau	29.12.17		1 Section Machine Gun Coy arrived from Base to complete Establishment. Lieut E.H.R. Shepherd assumed command of 173rd Coy & Coy.	
	30.12.17		Casualties for month of December. Officers killed 5, wounded 8, missing 2. Other Ranks killed 42, wounded 197, missing 40. Divisional Headquarters Staff. G.O.C. Major General R.W.R. Barnes C.B. D.S.O.; A.D.C. Capt H. S.G. Clowes (R.H.A.); A.D.C.-Lieut Commandant Capt J.B. J'Anvers; G.S.O. 1st Col J.R. Walters D.S.O.; G.S.O. 2nd Capt N.A.S. Alston M.C.; G.S.O. 3rd Capt R.E.C. Glyn; A.A.&Q.M.G. Lt Col W.M. Stewart; D.A.A.G. Major B.S. Moor Bludell D.S.O.; D.A.Q.M.G. Major H.C. Duke; A.D.M.S. Col T.F. Dewar C.B.; D.A.D.M.S. Capt M. S. King M.C.; D.A.D.V.S. Major P.W. Dagger Smith; A.P.M. Major W. Blazury; D.A.D.O.S. Captain R.L. Humphrys.	

M.C. Shuldstone
Br Gen
Cmdg 31st Divn

ORIGINAL.

WAR DIARY.

57th DIVISION.

"A" & "Q"

JANUARY 1918.

A + Q 57th Div
Army Form C. 2118.

WAR DIARY
or
INTELLIGENCE SUMMARY.
(Erase heading not required.)

Instructions regarding War Diaries and Intelligence Summaries are contained in F.S. Regs., Part II. and the Staff Manual respectively. Title pages will be prepared in manuscript.

Place	Date	Hour	Summary of Events and Information	Remarks and references to Appendices
ELVERDINGHE	1-1-18		Capt J.G.B Bragley Staff Captain 171st Inf Brigade appointed DAAG 62 Division	
	3-1-18		Divisional Headquarters removed from Elverdinghe Chateau to STEENWERCK	
STEENWERCK	4-1-18		Division transferred to XV Corps First Army.	
			Capt W.O. Lay Border Regiment appointed Staff Captain 171st Inf Brigade & reports for duty	
	16-1-18		Capt R.E.C. Glyn M.C. appointed GSO 2nd Grade H.Q XV Corps and leaves to take up appointment	
	18-1-18		Capt E.J de C Boys M.C Lincolnshire Regiment appointed G.S.O 3 of this Division and reports for duty	
	24-1-18		Instructions received relating to the reorganization of Infantry Brigade of this Division First Army Gen. Order No 1794 (G) dated 16 January 1918. G 614/57/1 dated 22 January 1918. Each Infantry Brigade to consist of three strong Battalions instead of four weak ones e) 1/4 Q and a nucleus of 1/12 Liverpool Regt. 1/9 Liverpool Regt. 2/1/5 Loyal North Lancs to be transferred from 55th Division and amalgamate with 2/5 Liverpool Regt 2/9 Liverpool Regt & 4/5 Loyal North Lancs The battalions thus formed to become the 2nd King's Liverpool Regt. & 5 Loyal North Lancs Regt. (b) 2/5 Scottish Rifles & 2/5 Liverpool Regt will be broken up & distributed amongst MG Battalions. (C) 2/5 Loyal North Lancs Regt will become a Pioneer Batt 57 Div. After reorganization complete Infantry Brigade will be as follows	

T2134. Wt. W708—776. 500000. 4/15. Sir J.C. & S.

WAR DIARY or INTELLIGENCE SUMMARY

Army Form C. 2118.

Place	Date	Hour	Summary of Events and Information	Remarks and references to Appendices
			170 Inf Brigade : 2/5 R Lancs Regt, 5th Loyal North Lancs, 2/4 Loyal North Lancs	
			171st Inf Brigade : 2/1 Liverpool Regt, 2/6 Liverpool Regt, 2/7 Liverpool Regt	
			172nd Inf Brigade : 9th Liverpool Regt, 2/10 Liverpool Regt, 2/4 S Lancs Regt	
			Pioneer Coy : 4/5 Loyal North Lancs	
	3.1.18		Transfer approved of Lieut J Tyrwhitt 5 Brum Chaplain 5y Div to X Corps for appointment as Assistant Adjutant General Corps	
	16.1.18		Reverend C E Burkett C of E appointed on dft. appointed Senior Chaplain of Division	
	26.1.18		Reinforcements from the 29th December 1917 to 26 January 1918 numbered 22 Officers 531 Other Ranks	
	31.1.18		Casualties for month of January 1918. Officers killed nil, wounded 9, missing nil, sick 31. Other Ranks killed 26, wounded 116, Self inflicted 3, missing 9, sick 1624. — Cases of Trench feet Officers 1. Other Ranks 189.	
			Div H.Q. staff GOC Major General R.J.R. Jeune CB SSO ADC Capt W St G Cluros (RJO) A/G Kamplen Capt J R L'Arvey GSO I Lt Col J R Welkes DSO GSO 2 Capt W H S A Bloome 9.20 3 Capt E J Boys MC ARAQMG LtColonel Steward DSO	
			DAAG Major B S Moss Blundell DSO Bn QMG Major H C Duke ADMS Col T F Dewar CB DADMS Capt MC King MC DADVS Major Du Deyn Smith APM Major W Blenary DADSS Capt B L Humphrys	

M.B. Winter Major
G.S.O.1
for Major General
Cmdg 57th Division

Army Form C. 2118.

HQ A + Q 57th DIVISION

Vol 13

WAR DIARY
or
INTELLIGENCE SUMMARY.
(Erase heading not required.)

Instructions regarding War Diaries and Intelligence Summaries are contained in F.S. Regs., Part II. and the Staff Manual respectively. Title pages will be prepared in manuscript.

Place	Date	Hour	Summary of Events and Information	Remarks and references to Appendices
STEENWERCK	5/2/18		Lieut Col J F R HOPE DSO appointed C.O. 57th Machine Gun Bn. Capt N S G MAYSER G.N. appointed adjutant	/nc
	6/7/18		In consequence of prevalence of French fret in the Division XV Corps call for report on certain cases A.D.M.S. makes report which is forwarded to the Corps.	/nc
	11.2.18		Lieut + QM H H BALL 9th KLIR appointed QM 57th Machine Gun Batn. Lieut J M Shepherd appointed Transport Officer.	/nc
MERVILLE	16.2.18		Divisional Head Quarters removed to Merville from STEENWERCK.	/nc
	20.2.18		Major W A GRIERSON DSO appointed Second in Command of 57th Machine Gun Batt.	/nc
	23.2.18		Lieut Col PARSONS late Col MACDONALD and Lieut Col BROOKE RAMC ordered to proceed home and report to the War Office (XV Corps A.C. 9186)	/nc
	24.2.18		Lieut W E A BLACKMAN (17 D.G. (oy) departs for 110 Machine Gun Coy	/nc
	25.2.18		Major A C H DUKE DAQMG departs to take up appointment of AAQMG 50th Division [Appendixed /2598/A.G. 9 24 Feb 1918]	/nc
	26.2.18		Major E P J STOURTON DSO Y.L.I appointed D A Q M G.	/nc
	27.2.18		The Surplus of 2/5 K & R and 2/5 South Lancs joined No 2 Entrenching Batn at DOULIEU	/nc
	28.2.18		Personnel of 57th Divl M G Batn Concentrated. Pioneer Batln formed on three Company Basis extra Personnel not sent away number being than 40 attachem	/nc
			Sickness in Division this month has been abnormally high.	/nc

WAR DIARY or INTELLIGENCE SUMMARY

Army Form C. 2118.

Place	Date	Hour	Summary of Events and Information	Remarks and references to Appendices
			Reinforcements for the month numbered 33 Officers and 1800 O.R.	
			Casualties for the month of February Officers killed Nil wounded 1 missing Nil Sick 13.	Ift
			Other Ranks killed 5 wounded 90 missing 2 self inflicted wounds 4 Sick 851. Exen at	Ift
			trend feet 9 O.R.	
			Div H.Q. Staff. G.O.C Major General R.N.R Reade CB DSO ADC Capt W Sr G Clowes (R of O) ADC	Ift
			+ Camp Commandant Capt J.B. L'Amery GSO¹ Lieut Col J R Nelter DSO GSO² Capt W H S Alston MC	
			G.S.O³ Capt E J Boyce MC. AA & QMG Lt Col W M Stewart DSO BA&G Major B S Mare Ahmad DSO	
			BAEMG. —— ADMS Col T F Dewar CR DADMS Capt W B King MC DADVS Major P W	
			Dyer Smith APM Major W Bleyney DADOS Capt B L Humphreys	

ORIGINAL

WAR DIARY.

HEADQUARTERS, 57th Division, "A" & "Q".

MARCH, 1918.

Army Form C. 2118.

WAR DIARY
or
INTELLIGENCE SUMMARY.
(Erase heading not required.)

A & Q 57th Division

Instructions regarding War Diaries and Intelligence Summaries are contained in F.S. Regs., Part II. and the Staff Manual respectively. Title pages will be prepared in manuscript.

Place	Date	Hour	Summary of Events and Information	Remarks and references to Appendices
Merville	2.3.18.		Captain A.W.B. Lowdon RAMC T.F. took over command of the 3/2 West Lancs Field Ambulance	JAL
	5.3.18.		Lieut Col P.T. Rutherford RAMC T.F. took over command of 2/2/2 Wessex Field Ambulance	JAL
	9.3.18.		Captain J.R.R. Trist M.C. RAMC S.R. took over command of 2/2 Wessex Field Ambulance	JAL
	9.3.18.		Major E.P.T. Stourton DSO reports for duty on appointment to DAQMG.	JAL
	9.3.18.		Summer time comes into force night of 9/10	JAL
	10.3.18.		In view of possibility of enemy attack on this front 171st Infantry Brigade move from NORRENT-FONTES Area to MERVILLE Area (Hqrs LES LAURIERS). 170 Infantry Brigade move from MERVILLE Area to Donlieu. 285th Brigade R.F.A. recalled from practice at WESTRENEM and return to wagon lines	JAL
			at HAVERSKERQUE GS03	JAL
	14.3.18		Capt E.J. De Boys M.C. goes to hospital. (sick)	JAL
Croix du Bac	21.3.18		Divisional Headquarters removed from MERVILLE to CROIX DU BAC.	JAL
	23.3.18		All leave stopped, except in special cases, until further orders	JAL
	26.3.18		Telegram sent to England recalling G.S.O.1 and C.R.A.	JAL
	28.3.18		Orders received to recall all Staff Officers on leave. Telegram despatches recalling Major Hugo Blundell DSO six	JAL
			H.Q. A&Q and Capt Tony Sky-Captain 171st Infantry Brigade	
			Reinforcements for the month numbered 14 Officers and 1340 Other Ranks	JAL

Army Form C. 2118.

A & Q 57 Division

WAR DIARY
or
INTELLIGENCE SUMMARY.
(Erase heading not required.)

Instructions regarding War Diaries and Intelligence Summaries are contained in F.S. Regs., Part II. and the Staff Manual respectively. Title pages will be prepared in manuscript.

Place	Date	Hour	Summary of Events and Information	Remarks and references to Appendices
			Casualties for month of March Officers killed 1 wounded 4 Missing Nil Sick 12; Other Ranks killed 38 wounded 233 Missing 1 self inflicted wounds 1 Sick 607 Cases of trench feet 3. O.R.	JVC
			Divisional H.Q. Staff G.O.C Major General R.H.R Barnes CB. D.S.O. ADC Capt W.B. & Clowes (R.90) ADC & Camp Commandant Capt J.B L'Armay. GSO 1 Lieut Col J.R. Hotblack D.S.O. GSO 2 Major W.H.S. Alston MC. GSO 3 Capt E.J. Boys MC AA+QMG Lt Col W.M Stewart DSO. DAAG Major B.E. Moss Blundell. ASC. DAQMG Major E.P.J. Stourton DSO. ADMS Col T.F Dewar CB. DADMS Capt M.B. King M.E. DADVS Major P.W Dwyer Smith APM Major W. Blayney. DADOS Capt R.L Humphrys	Jvl

Major General
Commanding 57 Division

Administrative 57th Div.

WAR DIARY

A. & Q.

57th DIVISION

APRIL 1918

"A" & "Q" BRANCH

HEADQUARTERS 57th DIVISION.

ORIGINAL WAR DIARY

APRIL 1918.

Army Form C. 2118.

A-Q 57th Division

WAR DIARY

(Erase heading not required.)

Instructions regarding War Diaries and Intelligence Summaries are contained in F. S. Regs., Part II. and the Staff Manual respectively. Title pages will be prepared in manuscript.

Place	Date	Hour	Summary of Events and Information	Remarks and references to Appendices
		1918		
		April		
Croix Du Bac	1		Divisional Headquarters removed to MERVILLE closing at 4 P.M.	
MERVILLE	2	"	Divisional Headquarters removed to LUCHEUX opening at 4 P.M. Division move from MERVILLE	
LUCHEUX	2	"	AREA b. train Entraining stations MERVILLE CALONNE and STEENBECQUE	
"	3	"	DETRAINING Stations DOULLENS and MONDICOURT	
"	5	"	Divisional Headquarters removed to COUTURELLE from LUCHEUX.	
"	8	"	2/Lieut (a/Capt) B.H Harrison Royal Munster Fusiliers appointed G.S.O 3 & 2/Lt Temp Capt Welsh to Camp Comdt.	AG.GHQ AM15/3104
COUTURELLE	9	"	Divisional Headquarters removed to BEAUQUESNE from COUTURELLE.	
BEAUQUESNE	12	"	Divisional Headquarters removed to LUCHEUX	
LUCHEUX	14	"	Divisional Headquarters removed to PAS Division in camps round PAS and AUTHIE	
PAS	19	"	2/10 Bn The King's Liverpool (Scottish) Regt transferred from 57th Division to 55th Division for amalgamation with 1/10 Bn The King's Liverpool (Scottish) Regt	
"	19	"	1st Bn Munster Fusiliers transferred from 16th Division to 57th Division to replace 2/10 Bn The King's Liverpool (Scottish) Regt	
"	24	"	Lt Col H.T Stokes A.S.C 57th Divisional Train appointed A.D.S+T IX Corps	
			(Authority QMG GHQ wire Q.P.2206 of 24th April 1918)	

Army Form C. 2118.

WAR DIARY

INTELLIGENCE SUMMARY.
(Erase heading not required.)

A.D. 57 Division (2)

Instructions regarding War Diaries and Intelligence Summaries are contained in F.S. Regs., Part II. and the Staff Manual respectively. Title pages will be prepared in manuscript.

Place	Date	Hour	Summary of Events and Information	Remarks and references to Appendices
PAS	1918			
	30 April		Major the E.P.J. Glascodine DADMS, appointed AADMS 25 Div	
	"		Capt. W.B. Wiltshire, Staff Capt. 101st Inf. Bde, appointed DADMS. 57th Div.	PAS
			Army IV Corps A/5104 30.4.18.	
			Casualties during month of April.	
			Off. Killed 1. Wounded 11 (incl 2 at duty) Missing 9. Sick 23	PAS
			O.R. " 28. " 154 (" 11 ") " 59 " 776	PAS
			S.I.W. Fifteen.	PAS
			Reinforcements during April Fifteen. 27 officers 1262 other ranks.	
			Divl HQ Staff	
			G.O.C. Maj-Gen R.W.R. Barnes, C.B. D.S.O.	
			A.D.C. Capt. W.F.E. Clowes (R.F.A.)	
			A.D.C. Camp Comm. Capt J.B. l'Army	
			G.S.O.1 Lieut-Col J.R. Whitehead D.S.O.	
			G.S.O.2 Major W.N.J. Aston M.C.	
			G.S.O.3 Capt. B. St. Denman M.C.	
			AAQMG. Lt-Col W. McSheehan D.S.O.	
			AAAG. Major B.S. McD. Blundell D.S.O.	
			ADMS. Lt-Col T.F. Dewan C.B.	
			ADVS. Major W.B. King M.C.	
			DADMS Major P.W. Raymond.	
			A.P.M. Major W. Blagrove	
			DADOS Capt. B.G. Humphreys	
			Sen Chap. Rev C.E. Burkitt	

Army Form C. 2118.

A + Q
57th Division

WAR DIARY
INTELLIGENCE SUMMARY.
(Erase heading not required.)

Instructions regarding War Diaries and Intelligence Summaries are contained in F. S. Regs., Part II. and the Staff Manual respectively. Title pages will be prepared in manuscript.

Place	Date	Hour	Summary of Events and Information	Remarks and references to Appendices
Pas	30/4 1918.		The Division has been at rest in Army and Corps reserve during the month and has been behind the VI Corps and IV Corps front. During the latter half of the month mostly the whole division has been under canvas. There were not enough huts to go round but the men learnt to make improvised cover out of hurdles in the woods where the camps were mostly situated around Pas and Antie. Although the weather was not April the bulk of the Division informed as now as the men went under canvas. Although the frequent moves and other recent conditions have had a harmful effect on the Division. Certainly all ranks were pleased to get out of the dull and damp country in Flanders and see the killer and pretty[?] country[?] of the Somme for the first time.

MA Mackesy[?] Mr
Major General
Comdg 57th Division | Pro |

ORIGINAL
WAR DIARY.
MAY
1918.

Headquarters 57th DIVISION.

"A" & "Q" Branch.

Army Form C. 2118.

WAR DIARY
INTELLIGENCE SUMMARY
(Erase heading not required.)

A & Q 57th Division

Place	Date	Hour	Summary of Events and Information	Remarks and references to Appendices
	1918			
PAS	1 May		Major N.R. Gibson S.S.O. 57th Division assumed duty on appointment to command 57th Divisional Train	
"	1 "		R.C. Chaplain J. Flynn, attached 10th Battn. Royal Munster Fusiliers left on 1/5/18 to report to VI Corps H.A.	
"	5 "		T/Major N.B. White D.S.O. M.C. Gen. List, assumed duty as D.A.Q.M.G. (Auty.) A.Q. 266. 30.4.18	
"	5 "		Capt (T/Major) W.K.S. Alston M.C. D.S.O. 2 appointed D.S.O. 2 VII Corps (Auty H.Q.) 2965 dated 1.5.18	
"	5 "		Capt. R.S. Van R. in Shurm D.S.O. M.C. Hampshire Regt. appointed D.S.O. 2 57th Division vice N.B. White to be T/Major. Assumed duty as D.S.O. 2 5.5.18 (Auty A.Q. 2965 dated 1.5.18	
"	6 "		Relieved 42 Division in Corps Division Sector IV Corps. Divisional H.Q. closing at 4 pm PAS, reopening same hour at COUIN.	
COUIN	7 "		Capt. N.S.S. J. Manciegh M.C. appointed to O.C. 57 Bn Machine Gun Corps vice Major R.A. Wade to 46th Bn Machine Gun Corps	
"	9 "		Capt. B.H. Harrison M.C. D.S.O. 3 wounded	

Army Form C. 2118.

WAR DIARY

INTELLIGENCE SUMMARY.

(Erase heading not required.)

Instructions regarding War Diaries and Intelligence Summaries are contained in F.S. Regs., Part II. and the Staff Manual respectively. Title pages will be prepared in manuscript.

Place	Date	Hour	Summary of Events and Information	Remarks and references to Appendices
	1918			
COUIN	May 10		Lieut. J.P. Hartworth appointed G.S.O.3. 57th Division as from 10.5.18 vice Capt. R.H. Harrison. M.C. wounded 9.5.18	
"	"		Major G.O.L. Rae. 10th Bn. King's Liverpool Regt. attached 9th King's L'pool Rgt. posted to 7th Bn. Manchester Regiment with effect from 9.5.18.	
"	17		Major J.B. Sindall relinquished the command of 505th Field Company R.E. and Major R.L. Jordan assumed command of 505 Field Coy R.E. 17.5.18	
"	20		C.E. Chaplain C.S. Sweeny, attached to 57th Division H.Q. from 20/5/18 vice C.E. Chaplain R.J. Porthcott, wounded (gas)	
"	30		Reinforcements for tunnels 37 Officers and 1365 O.R.	
"	31		Casualties for tunnels Officers killed 2 wounded 19 wounded (gas) 33 Injured 1 Sick 50. Other Ranks Killed 62 wounded 364 wounded (gas) 592. died of wounds 2 Injured 8. Self inflicted wounds 10. Missing 2 Sick 1362 Divisional H.Q. Staff. G.O.C. Major Gen. R.W.R. Barnes C.B. D.S.O. A.D.C. and Camp Commandant Capt. J.B. Yarmouth. - G.S.O.1. Lt. Col. G.R. Metheuen D.S.O. G.S.O.2. Major B.B. Von Thurn. - G.S.O.3 Capt. J.P. Hartworth.	

T2134. W. W708-776. 500000. 4/15. Sir J.C.&S.

WAR DIARY
or
INTELLIGENCE SUMMARY.

Army Form C. 2118.

Place	Date	Hour	Summary of Events and Information	Remarks and references to Appendices
	1918			
COULIY	31 May		A.A.&Q.M.G. Lt. Col. W.M. Stewart. DSO. — D.A.A.G. Major B.S. Moss-Blundell DSO. D.A.Q.M.G. — Major W.B. White DSO, MC. — A.D.M.S. Col. J.F. Denoon C.B. AMS. D.A.D.M.S. — Capt. W.B. King. MC. (RAMC) D.A.D.V.S. Major P.K. Bayes-Smith AVC. D.A.D.O.S. Capt. R.J. Humphreys A.O.D. — A.P.M. Major W. Blayney. and Senior Chaplain Rev. C.E. Curtitt.	

Mb Shelmerm
Major General
Commanding 57th Division

57TH DIVISION.

SECRET.   **LOCATION LIST.**   1st June, 1918.

	Locality.	Map Reference Sheet. Sheet 57d.
57th Divisional Headquarters.	COUIN.	J.1.b.5.0.
Royal Artillery.		
57th Div. Arty. Headquarters.	COUIN.	J.1.b.5.0.
H.Q. 210th Bde R.F.A.		E.8.c.7.3.
-do- (Wagon Lines)		D.27.d.4.8.
H.Q. 211th Bde R.F.A.		E.8.c.7.1.
-do- (Wagon Lines)		D.22.a.8.5.
H.Q. 310th Bde R.F.A.		J.6.a.6.3.
-do- (Wagon Lines)		C.30.d. & J.1.a.central.
H.Q. 312th Bde R.F.A.	AUTHIE	
-do- (Wagon Lines)		J.1.c.central.
H.Q. 285th Bde R.F.A.(Wagon Lines)		C.22.a.5.9.
H.Q. 286th Bde R.F.A. (-do-)		J.18.a.1.6.
H.Q. 42nd D.A.C. (do-)		J.1.d.9.0.
H.Q. 57th D.A.C. (-do-)		D.20.a.1.0.
H.Q. 62nd D.A.C. (-do-)		I.11.d.5.8.
H.Q. 42nd D.T.M.O.	COUIN.	
H.Q. 57th D.T.M.O.		J.10.b.55.85.
57th Divisional Engineers.		
Headquarters.	COUIN.	J.1.b.central.
421st Field Coy., R.E. (H.Q.)		E.28.d.70.65.
-do- (Transport.)		J.3.b.1.5.
502nd Field Coy., R.E.	COIGNEUX.	J.3.b.3.4.
-do-	GOMMECOURT WOOD	E.28.central.
505th Field Coy., R.E.	GOMMECOURT WOOD	E.28.c.98.70
-do- (Transport)	COIGNEUX.	J.9.a.4.2.
170th Infantry Brigade.		
Headquarters.	COUIN.	J.1.b.4.7.
2/5th K.O.R.Lancs.R. (Adv)	Ch.de la HAIE.	J.6.b.07.79.
-do- (Rear.)	COIGNEUX.	J.9.a.45.30.
-do- (Transport)	COIGNEUX.	J.8.b.95.60.
2/4th L.N.Lancs. R.	BEER TRENCH.	E.28.c.2.4.
-do- (Transport)		J.8.b.3.2.
1/5th L.N.Lancs. R.	COIGNEUX.	J.3.c.90.55.
170th L.T.M.Bty.	BAYENCOURT.	J.10.b.45.95.
171st Infantry Brigade.		
Headquarters. (Adv.)	In Line.	
-do- (Rear)	COUIN.	J.7.a.7.6.
2/6th Liverpool Regt.	In Line.	K.4.a.2.4.
-do- (Transport)	COUIN.	J.7.a.85.75.
2/7th Liverpool Regt.	In Line.	K.4.b.60.15.
-do- (Transport)	COUIN.	J.7.a.6.8.
8th Liverpool Regt.	In Line.	E.28.d.5.1.
-do- (Transport)	COUIN.	J.7.a.7.6.
171st L.T.M.B.	FONQUEVILLERS.	K.4.b.2.6.
-do-	COIGNEUX.	J.2.b.65.20.
172nd Infantry Brigade.		
Headquarters. (Adv.)	FONQUEVILLERS.	E.27.a.85.60.
-do- (Rear)	COIGNEUX.	J.9.a.3.8.
1st Royal Munster Fus.		K.6.a.15.05.
-do- (Transport)		J.3.c.
9th Liverpool Regt.		E.29.a.3.7.
-do- (Transport)		J.3.c.
2/4th South Lancs. Regt.		K.6.a.4.4.
-do- (Transport)		K.3.c.
172nd L.T.M.Bty.		E.28.d.1.

P.T.O.

(2)

	Locality.	Map Reference Sheet. Sheet 57d.
57th Bn. M. G. Corps.		
Headquarters.	COUIN.	J.1.d.5.5.
Transport Lines.	do	J.2.b.10.27.
"A" Company. (Rear H.Q.)	do	J.2.b.0.2.
"B" Company. (-do-)	do	J.2.b.0.2.
"C" Company. (-do-)	do	J.2.b.0.2.
"D" Company. (-do-)	do	J.2.d.2.3.
"A" Company. (Adv. H.Q.)	GOMMECOURT.	E.29.a.56.20.
"B" Company. -do-	GOMMECOURT.	E.28.d.35.92.
"C" Company. -do-	HEBUTERNE.	K.3.c.4.1.
"D" Company. (-do-)		J.2.d.2.3.
2/5th L.N.Lancs. R. (P)	COIGNEUX.	J.3.c.40.15.
-do- (Transport)	COIGNEUX.	J.3.c.15.15.
57th Div.Sig.Coy. R.E.	COUIN.	J.1.d.4.8.
57th Divisional Train.		
Headquarters.	COUIN.	L.25.d.9.0.
No. 1 Company.	do	I.6.c.8.6.
No. 2 Company.	do	J.1.b.7.9.
No. 3 Company.	AUTHIE.	I.17.b.8.8.
No. 4 Company.	do	I.17.a.4.5.
2/2nd Wessex Field Ambce.	SOUASTRE.	D.22.c.6.3.
-do- (Transport)	COUIN.	J.1.c.0.3.
2/3rd Wessex Field Ambce.	SOUASTRE.	D.22.c.6.3.
-do- (Transport)	COUIN.	J.1.c.1.3.
3/2nd West Lancs. Fd. Amb.	COUIN.	J.1.b.6.7.
-do- (Transport)	COUIN.	J.1.b.8.8.
57th M. T. Company.	PAS-GRINCOURT Road.	
D.A.D.O.S.	COUIN.	
D.A.D.V.S.	COUIN.	
57th Mob.Vet.Section.	PAS.	C.17.c.2.2.
57th Railhead Camp.	COUIN.	
Claims Officer.	COUIN.	
Salvage & Burials Officer.	COUIN.	
57th Divisional Wing.	MARIEUX.	

DISTRIBUTION TO :-

170th Inf. Bde.	A.D.M.S.	No.3 Sec. D.A.C.
171st Inf. Bde.	57th Div. Train.	57th M.Vet.Sec.
172nd Inf. Bde.	57th M.T.Coy.	A?P:M:
2/5th L.N.L.R.	57th R'Head Camp.	Camp Commandant.
57th Bn. M.G.C.	57th Div'l Wing.	"G".
C.R.A.	D.A.D.O.S.	"Q".
C.R.E.	D.A.D.V.S.	Senior Chaplain.
57th Div.Sig.Coy.	R.T.O.WARLINCOURT.	Postal Services.
R.T.O. DOULLENS.	Claims Officer.	Salvage Officer.
Baths Officer.	Gas Officer.	

1st June, 1918.

Major,
D.A.A.G. 57th Division.

C.R.A.,

    57th Division.

       On the Divisional Artillery rejoining the Division after taking part in the recent battle on the Lys, the Divisional Commander, in the name of the Division, wishes to thank them for the way in which they upheld the name of the Division.   The G.O.C., R.A. XV Corps, and the G.O.Cs. 31st and 40th Divisions have all testified in writing on the gallant and efficient manner in which they carried out their duties; the command of the D.A. and the handling of the Brigades have also been mentioned as excellent.

                                                                    Lieut-Colonel,

D.H.Q.
11/5/1918.
                                     A.A.& Q.M.G., 57th Division.

Copies to:-   170th Inf.Brigade.
               171st Inf.Brigade.
               172nd Inf.Brigade.
               all Inf.Battalions.
               C.R.E.,
               Signals.
               2/5th L.N.L.R.(P).
               57th Bn.M.G.Corps.
               Divisional Train.
               A.D.M.S.

Vol 17

June 1918

War Diary

"A" & "Q"

57 Divn

Original

Army Form C. 2118.

WAR DIARY
~~INTELLIGENCE SUMMARY.~~
(Erase heading not required.)

Headquarters
57th Division A & Q

Instructions regarding War Diaries and Intelligence Summaries are contained in F.S. Regs., Part II. and the Staff Manual respectively. Title pages will be prepared in manuscript.

Place	Date	Hour	Summary of Events and Information	Remarks and references to Appendices
	1918			
COUIN	1 June		Lieut. Col. G.H. Cawley, K.S.L.I, assumed command of the 7/5 The King's Own Royal Lancaster Regiment on 30.5.18	JRO
"	1 "		Chaplain W.M. Thomson, United Board, posted to 3/y West Lancs Field Ambulance	JRO
"	8 "		Lieut. Col. J.J. Cameron D.S.O. M.C. 7/5 The King's Own Royal Lancaster Regt, proceeded to England	JRO
"	9 "		57th Divisional Reception Camp formed and Capt. M.K. Birch appointed Commandant	JRO
"	15 "		Chaplain J.A. Jagoe O.B.E. reported for duty with 2/4 South Lancashire Regt.	JRO
"	17 "		Q/M and Hon'y Lieut. S. Sutherland posted to 5/7 King's Liverpool Regt.	JRO
"	19 "		Capt. W.H. Dawson 2/4 Loyal North Lancashire Regt. appointed Divisional Educational Officer and assumed duties 19.6.18	JRO
"	27 "		Chaplain W.E. Smith, C.T.E. to England on expiration of contract	JRO
"	28 "		Lieut. G.H. Jasper, arrived as adjutant of 57th Divisional Reception Camp	JRO
"	29 "		Inspection by Medical Inspector of Drafts, of officers and other ranks for reclassification at Marieux.	JRO
"	29 "		T/Major B.L. Humphrys vacated appointment as DADOS	JRO

WAR DIARY

Place	Date	Hour	Summary of Events and Information	Remarks and references to Appendices
COUIN	1918 June 29		T/Capt. C.M. Moser assumed duties as DADOS. Casualties for the month of June :- Killed: Officers 4, O/Ranks 61, Wounded - Officers 16, O/Ranks 299. Wounded at duty: Officers 7, O/Ranks 49. Missing - Officers 2 (wounded missing) O/Ranks 9. Gassed - Officers 2, O/Ranks 2.S. Injuries self inflicted - O/Ranks 9. Sick :- Officers 46, O/Ranks 1384. Total reinforcements for June. Officers 59, O/Ranks 1352.	JAO
"	30		Divisional Hdqrs. Pro Staff. ADC and Camp Commandant Capt. J.B. Jarvey. ASO.I B.T.Col J.C. Nethern. DSO. GSO 2 Capt. (T/Major) R.S. vou Dieur Dem Jeuxy DSO, MC. GSO 3. Lieut. (T/Capt.) J.P. Nasmyth. ADMS. Major (T/Lt Col) W.M. Shergolt. DSO. I. Major B.S. Mrs-Blunsell. OBE, DSO. DAAG. T/Major N.B. White. DSO. MC. RCMS. DAQMG. Lt & Major G.R. Smith. DADMS. Capt. (T/Major) M.D. King. MC. RAMC. DADOT T/Capt. CM Moser. DADVS T/Major P.W. Sayer. SMRC. AVC. APM. T/Major N. Blaney and Senior Chaplain. Rev. CE Burkitt.	JAO

M. Whiter Major
for Major General
Commanding 57 Division

WAR DIARY
INTELLIGENCE SUMMARY
(Erase heading not required.)

Army Form C. 2118.

AO 090 57D

Vol 18

Place	Date	Hour	Summary of Events and Information	Remarks and references to Appendices
	1918			
COUIN	1 July		Major-General R.W.R. BARNES CB, DSO proceeds to ENGLAND on leave and Brigadier J.C. WRAY CMG MVO RA assumes command of 57th Division during his absence	
"	2 "		57th Division is relieved by the NEW ZEALAND Division and moves into CORPS Reserve. 57th Divisional Headquarters move to AUTHIE. A and Q Offices close at COUIN at 4 pm at AUTHIE at 4 pm	
AUTHIE	4 "		Captain G. McDONALD MC - Staff Captain 170 th Infy Bde - proceeds to 37th Division for duty as Acting DAAG of that Division. Captain J.H. ORTNER - 2/5 Bn The King's Own Royal Lancaster Regt - assumes duty as Acting Staff Captain 170th Infy Bde.	
"	11 "		Lieut-Colonel H.W.P. STOKES DSO, ASC assumes command of 57th Divisional Train vice Major A/Lt Colonel W.R. GIBSON DSO, ASC.	
"	14 "		Captain A/Major R.E. VYVYAN RE (Signals) proceeds to ENGLAND for duty and Captain J.S. PHIPPS RE assumes duty as OC 57th Divisional Signal Coy	

WAR DIARY

INTELLIGENCE SUMMARY. (2)

Army Form C. 2118.

Place	Date	Hour	Summary of Events and Information	Remarks and references to Appendices
	1918			
AUTHIE	15 July		Lieut Colonel H.W.P. STOKES DSO ASC is ordered to GHQ for duty there and Major A/Lieut Colonel W.R. GIBSON DSO ASC assumes command of 57th Divisional Train.	
	16		57th Division moves to PAS. A/Q Offices close at AUTHIE at 4 pm and open at PAS 4 pm. Major General R.W.R. BARNES CB DSO returns from leave and reassumes command of 57th Division. Brigadier General F.G. GUGGISBERG CMG DSO relinquishes command of the 170th Infy Brigade and Brigadier General G.F. BOYD CMG DSO DCM assumes command of that Brigade.	
PAS	17		Lieut-Colonel Lord H/C. SEYMOUR DSO - Grenadier Guards - assumes command of the 9th Bn "The King's" (Liverpool Regt) vice Captain A/Lt Colonel S.C. BALL MC - 5th Bn The King's Own Royal Lancaster Regt - who reverts to 2nd in command of the 9th Bn "The King's" (Liverpool Regt)	
	21 } 22 }		57th Divisional Horse Show was held at I 6 c Central (near St LEGER-LES-AUTHIE). Everything was arranged within the Division including the cooking of food for refreshments. Approximately 8,000 Officers and men had refreshment-	

WAR DIARY

INTELLIGENCE SUMMARY.

Army Form C. 2118.

(3)

Place	Date	Hour	Summary of Events and Information	Remarks and references to Appendices
	1918			
PAS	21 July		on the 21st and 9,000 Officers and men on the 22nd. The weather was good and the show was a great success. Programme and list of winners attached.	
	22			
	23		Lieut-Colonel W.A.L. FLETCHER DSO relinquishes command of the 2/6 KRR "The King's" (Liverpool Regt) and proceeds on leave in FRANCE pending transfer to ENGLAND. Major the Hon. N.C. GATHORNE-HARDY - Rifle Bde - assumes command of the 2/6 KRR "The King's" Liverpool Regt.	
	26		Lieut Al[strikethrough] A/Major B.L. HUMPHRYS Army Ordnance Dept assumes duty as the SADOS 57th Division vice T/Captain A/Major C.W. MESSER Army Ordnance Dept who proceeds to 2nd Division for further instruction in the duties of a DADOS.	
	29		57th Division is relieved by 63rd RN Division. 57th Division moves from IV Corps area to VI Corps area, with Divisional Headquarters at BOUQUEMAISON. A+Q Offices close at PAS at 11am and open at BOUQUEMAISON at 11am.	
BOUQUE-MAISON	30		57th Division moves from VI Corps area to XVII Corps area with AP & Qr at HERMAVILLE. A+Q Offices close at BOUQUEMAISON at 11am and open at HERMAVILLE at 11am.	

Army Form C. 2118.

WAR DIARY
INTELLIGENCE SUMMARY
(Erase heading not required.)

Place	Date	Hour	Summary of Events and Information	Remarks and references to Appendices
	1918 30 July		Casualties for the month of July:- Killed O/Ranks 7. Wounded Officers 1. O/Ranks 31. Injured O/Ranks 7. Injured self-inflicted O/Ranks 2. Sick Officers 18 O/Ranks 717. Total reinforcements for July Officers 51 O/Ranks 957. Divisional Headquarters Staff. G.O.C. Major General RWR Barnes CB DSO. A.D.C. and Camp Commandant Captain J.B. J'arnay. G.S.O, 1st Lt. Colonel J.R. Wethered DSO. G.S.O, Capt (T/Major) B.B. von B. em Thurn DSO MC G.S.O 3 Lieut (T/Captain) J.P. Wattlewrith. A.A. & Q.M.G. Major (T/Lt.Col) W.M. Stewart DSO. D.A. & Q Major B.S. Morris-Blundell DSO OBE D.A.Q.M.G. T/Major H.B. White DSO. M.C. ADMS Lt.Col (T/Col) Y.H. Seward CB AMS DADMS Capt (T/Major) Mr. B. King MCRAMC DADOS Lieut (A/Major) B.L. HUMPHREYS DADVS T/Major P.W. Sayer-Smith A.V.C. A.P.M. T/Major H. Blaney and Senior Chaplain D.C.G's Dept Rev C.E. Burkitt.	J. WB Hunt Captain Acting Staff Captain Commanding 5th Division

ORIGINAL

WAR DIARY.

"A" & "Q" BRANCH.

57th Division.

August 1918.

Army Form C. 2118.

WAR DIARY
or
INTELLIGENCE SUMMARY.

(Erase heading not required.)

57 Div. "A" "Q"
Aug. 1918.

Instructions regarding War Diaries and Intelligence Summaries are contained in F.S. Regs., Part II. and the Staff Manual respectively. Title pages will be prepared in manuscript.

Place	Date	Hour	Summary of Events and Information	Remarks and references to Appendices
	August			
HERMAVILLE	2		57 Div. relieved 4th Canadian Div. centre sector XVII Corps front. Div. H.Q. remaining	
ETRUN	2		to ETRUN, units accommodated ETRUN – ANZIN – ST CATHERINES – AGNEZ-les-DUISANS area.	
	8		Major (A/Lt Col) C.H. CAUTLEY Shrops Light Inf. comdg. 1/5 K.O.R.L.R. evacuated to sick. Divn. agreement 1st Shrops Lgn. Bn. (Army First Army A.F./2159/A3p.5 (Q) 3.8.18.)	
			2/Major F.J. POPHAM L.N.L. Regt. appointed to command 1/5 K.O.R.L.R.	
			A/(Capt) B.H. PERL M.C. 1/5 K.O.R.L.R appointed 2i/c 1/5 K.O.R.L.R.	
			Lieut Col (T/Brig Genl) W.C.E RUDKIN CMG D.S.O took over command 57 D.A	
	16		and Col (T/Brig Genl) J.C. WRAY CMG MVO (Lt Eng)	
			Arty. A.G. Appx/4155 15.8.18.	
	18		51 Div. relieved 57 Div (less 170 Bde remaining under orders of 51 Div).	
CHELERS	19		57 Div. H.Q. moved to CHELERS.	
	21		57 Div. (less 170 Bde) transferred from XVII Corps to VI Corps	
	22		170 Bde rejoined 57 Div.	
REBREUVE	23		57 Div. O.K.D. moved to REBREUVE.	
BAVINCOURT	24		57 Div. H.Q. moved to BAVINCOURT ; 57th Div transferred from VI Corps to XVII Corps	

WAR DIARY or INTELLIGENCE SUMMARY

Army Form C. 2118.

57 Div (A.Q) canvas

Place	Date	Hour	Summary of Events and Information	Remarks and references to Appendices
	1918 Aug			
BRETENCOURT	27		57 Div D.H.Q moved to BRETENCOURT – near Skops Camp Junction BASSEUX.	
MERCATEL	27		57 Divl. Hdrs. relieved 52 Div. in Corps Sector. XVII Corps – Divl. H.Q. moving to MERCATEL.	
	28		Rear H.Q. moved to BOIREVILLE	
	29	12 noon	172 Inf Bde attacked & captured HENDECOURT	
		1 pm	170 do. attacked & captured RIENCOURT and consequent on a strong enemy counter attack had to withdraw to line west of HENDECOURT during the evening.	
	31		Casualties for the month of August. Killed Officers 11 O/Ranks 136. Wounded Officers 41 O/Ranks 1009. Wounded at duty Officers 4 O/Ranks 15. Missing Officers 2 O/Ranks 116. Injured O/Ranks 10. Injured S.I. O/Ranks 6. Sick Officers 17 O/Ranks 723. Total reinforcements received during August Officers 64 O/Ranks 742. Divisional Headquarters Staff. G.O.C. Major General R.W.R. Barnes CB DSO A.D.C. and Camp Commandant Captain J.B. Jarmay. G.S.O. Br. Lt-Colonel	

Army Form C. 2118.

WAR DIARY
INTELLIGENCE SUMMARY
(Erase heading not required.)

Place	Date	Hour	Summary of Events and Information	Remarks and references to Appendices
	1918 August 31st		J.R Wethered DSO. GSO, Capt (T/Major) B.B. von B. in Thurn DSO M.C. GSO3 Lieut (T/Captain) J.P. Wattlewath. AA & QMG Major (T/Lt Colonel) W.Mc. Stewart DSO. DAQG Major B.S. Mon. Blundell DSO. OBE. DAAG T/Major H.B. White DSO. M.C. ADMS Lt Colonel (T/Colonel) T.J Derrat CB AMS DADMS Captain (T/Major) M.B. King MC RAMC DADOS Lieut (A/Major) B.L. Humphreys Sr. DJS T/Major J.W Fryer. Smith AVC. APM T/Major H Blarey and Senior Chaplain to C.G's Dept Rev. C.E. Burkitt	

(Sgd) M.B.Phelp Major SAA
for Major General
Commanding 57th Division.

ORIGINAL

WAR DIARY.

September, 1918.

57th DIVISION.

"A" & "Q" BRANCH.

Army Form C. 2118.

WAR DIARY
INTELLIGENCE SUMMARY.
(Erase heading not required.)

57th Division
A & Q

Instructions regarding War Diaries and Intelligence Summaries are contained in F. S. Regs., Part II. and the Staff Manual respectively. Title pages will be prepared in manuscript.

Place	Date	Hour	Summary of Events and Information	Remarks and references to Appendices
	September 1918			
BLAIRVILLE	3		Captain R.M. LAVERTON, Royal Fusiliers, reports for duty and is attached to 171st Infy Bde	
"	4		Brig.-Gen. A.L. RANSOME D.S.O. M.C. reports for duty as G.O.C. 170th Infy Bde	
"	4		Lt.-Col. T.H.S. MARCHANT D.S.O. relinquishes command of 2/4th 13th South Lancashire Regt, having been appointed to command 126th Infy Bde	
"	5		Brig.-Gen. G.F. BOYD DSO relinquishes command of 170th Infy Bde having been appointed to command 46th Division	
"	5		A/Major W. McCLURE appointed to command 2/4th 13th South Lancashire Regt temporarily vice Lt.-Col. T.H.S. MARCHANT D.S.O.	
"	10		A/Lt.-Col. E.B. COTTER D.S.O. relinquishes command of 286th Bde R.F.A. and is posted to the R.G.A. for duty.	
"	10		Major L.J.W. ROBINSON D.S.O. assumes command of 286th Bde RFA vice Major A/Lt.-Col. E.B. COTTER D.S.O.	
"	12		A office moves to QUEANT at 2.30 p.m. Q office moves to Adv. Div. HQ between QUEANT and CAGNICOURT	

Army Form C. 2118.

WAR DIARY
of
INTELLIGENCE SUMMARY.
(Erase heading not required.)

57th Division
A & Q

Instructions regarding War Diaries and Intelligence Summaries are contained in F. S. Regs., Part II. and the Staff Manual respectively. Title pages will be prepared in manuscript.

Place	Date	Hour	Summary of Events and Information	Remarks and references to Appendices
	September 1918			
BLAIRVILLE	12		Captain J.F. HOLT, 12th Div. Signal Coy arrives and assumes command of 57th Div. Signal Coy RE vice Captain A/Major J.F. PHIPPS	
	14		A/Major J.F. PHIPPS, late O/C 57th Div Signal Coy RE proceeds to 12th Div. Signal Coy RE as second in command.	
QUEANT	15		Lieut A/Major J.S. SECKER Commanding 421st W.Lancs Field Coy RE wounded	
"	17		57th Division moves to BAVINCOURT. A and Q offices close 10 AM and open at BAVINCOURT 10 A.M.	
BAVINCOURT	18		Captain Hon P.E. THELLUSSON, West Kent Yeomanry reports for duty as A.D.C. to G.O.C. 57th Division.	
"	23		Lt.Col J.F.R. HOPE D.S.O. relinquishes command of 57th B~ M.G.C. on being appointed to command 50th Infy Bde.	
"	23		Captain G. McLEAN 123rd Field Coy RE arrives and assumes command of 421st W Lancs Field Coy RE vice Lieut A/Major J.S. SECKER	
"	24		T/Major B.H. PUCKLE. D.S.O. 16th B~ M G C assumes command of 57th B~ MGC vice Lt Col J.F.R. HOPE DSO	

Army Form C. 2118.

WAR DIARY

INTELLIGENCE SUMMARY.

(Erase heading not required.)

57 Division
A + Q

Place	Date	Hour	Summary of Events and Information	Remarks and references to Appendices
	September 1918			
BAVINCOURT	26		A Office moves to QUEANT. A and Q Offices move to near PRONVILLE. A and Q offices close at BAVINCOURT at 4 p.m. and open near QUEANT and PRONVILLE respectively at 4 p.m.	
QUEANT	27		Captain G C M MILLER A P M No4 (St ALBANS) Area Eastern Command is attached for 14 days instruction in Traffic Control duties.	
	28		A office moves to near PRONVILLE. A office close at QUEANT at 5.30 p.m. and opens near PRONVILLE at 5.30 p.m.	
NR PRONVILLE	30		A and Q office move to E 28 b 2.7. (Map 20,000 Sheet 57c NE) A and Q Office close near PRONVILLE at 10 AM and open at E 28 b 2.7. at 10 AM. Total reinforcements received during September Officers 90 O/Ranks 1582. Casualties for the month of September. Killed Officers 30 O/Ranks 319 Wounded Officers 84 O/Ranks 1909 Missing Officers 2 O/Ranks 184 Injured:- Officers 3 O.Rs 24 ; Inj S.I. O.Rs 10 ; Sick #25 O.Rs 812.	

Divl 2.0. Sixty

G.O.C. Major General R.W.R. Barnes CB DSO
A.D.C. Capt. Hon P E THELLUSON. W Kent Yeo. Capt J B JANNEY (Essex Comm)
G.S.O. Br/Col J R WELEKER D.S.O.

WAR DIARY

INTELLIGENCE SUMMARY.
(Erase heading not required.)

Army Form C. 2118.

5th Division
A+Q

Place	Date	Hour	Summary of Events and Information	Remarks and references to Appendices
			G.S.O.3. Capt (T/Major) B.B. van B. in Thun. DSO M.C.	
			G.S.O.3. Lieut (T/Col) J.R. Wadsworth.	
			A.A.Q.M.G. Major (T/Col) Armstrong DSO	
			D.A.A.G. Major R.S. Mead Blundell DSO O.B.E	
			D.A.Q.M.G. T/Major W.B. White DSO M.C.	
			A.D.M.S. Lt Col (T/Col) J.T. Dunn C.B. A.M.S.	
			A.D.V.S. Capt (T/Major) M.B. King M.C. R.A.M.C.	
			D.A.D.O.S. Lieut (A/Major) B.L. Humphreys.	
			D.A.D.V.S. T/Major O.W. Dwyer Smith A.V.C.	
			S.C. D.C.A. Dept Rev C.R. Buckin	

Signed: MM Rhodes Morgan
Major
Commanding 5th Division

Vol 21

Original
War Diary
October
"A" & "Q"
54 Division

WAR DIARY
or
INTELLIGENCE SUMMARY.
(Erase heading not required.)

Army Form C. 2118.

57th Div. A+Q
Oct, 1918. (1)

Place	Date	Hour	Summary of Events and Information	Remarks and references to Appendices
Near Cambrai	3rd		Lt. Col. In. E. Magill-Crichton-Maitland DSO. Assumed Command after to command of 9th K. Right. Regt.	PAO
	4th		Bde. Bn. Gn. B. Pompher DSO cmdg 172nd Bde. and Capt. C. V. Fisher-Rowe Mc. Bde. Major 172nd Bde wounded while hunt in camp.	MO
	5th		Gill Rox killing and wounding all occupants. Bde. Gen. F. C. Longbourne DSO cmdg 171st Bde. and Lt. Col. H. Ja Turke Camplese CRE wounded.	PAO
	9th		Capt T.W. Ogilvam after Bde Major 172nd Bde. May RC Leonard DSo Royal Scots Regt. after to command McMurdrie Tyndin	PAO
	9th		Troops of the Division entered Cambrai which was burning extensively in the centre of the town.	PAO
	11th		Bde-Gen Og Imermee CMG after to command 171st Bde.	APO
Boulin	12th		Headquarters of the Division moved to Boulin where the Division were well concentrated. Moved by trains which took many hours over three lines, owing to the discomfort of the troops. Came under 1st Corps 1st Army	PMO.

WAR DIARY
or
INTELLIGENCE SUMMARY

Army Form C. 2118.

57th Div. A + Q

Oct 1918

Place	Date	Hour	Summary of Events and Information	Remarks and references to Appendices
Barlin	12th		The Division continued to concentrate in this district. It was noticed that the spirit of the troops was excellent after their successes in the Cambrai battle.	
Epinette	14th		The Division concentrated around La Gorgue and Lestrem to take on the line for 47th Division moving to hold the Aubers area. The sector taken over was that of Fromelles and Aubers lines well beyond the old line held by the Division during the summer of 1917.	
Fromelles Englos	17th		Divisional HQ moved up to Englos. Fromelles. Our troops advanced to Lille and in evening 17th picquetted the outskirts of the town. Everywhere they were received with the greatest enthusiasm by the inhabitants who appeared overjoyed. The whole town was befloraged. Cars which stopped in the streets were surrounded by a crowd of both sexes who were eager to shake hands and in some cases kiss the deliverers.	
	18th		Div Headquarters moved to Englos.	

WAR DIARY or INTELLIGENCE SUMMARY

Army Form C. 2118.

57 Div HQ. A & Q
(3) Oct 1918

Place	Date	Hour	Summary of Events and Information	Remarks and references to Appendices
Ronchin	19th		Div Hq moved to Ronchin S. of Lille being billeted by the inhabitants with the same kindness.	190
"	20th		Major TD L Jordan RE. after CRE to Division	190
Willems	21st		Div Hq moved up to Willems about 4.7 miles west of Tournai.	190
"	22nd		Major C.W. Wilson 2nd in Cmd 6 KLR. transferred to T.F. Reserve at present to England	190
"	24th		Capt H.M. Rogers 3rd Shropshire L.I. att DAPM to Div	190
"	29th		Major F. Eames DSO 2/5 L.N.L. after to Command 18th Scottish Rifles	190
"	30th		Capt G. McDonald Gen Staff Capt 170 Bde after Davies 12th Divn	190
"	30th		Major C.T. Bampton DSO 285" Bde RFA after adv Bde	190
"	30th		Major 31st Div Arty	190
"	31st		Maj-Gen Barnes CB DSO awarded French Croix de Guerre	190
"	31st		Major Camplin DSO Bethune RA after Gfroji RA 7th Corps	190

WAR DIARY
or
INTELLIGENCE SUMMARY.

(Erase heading not required.)

Army Form C. 2118.

Oct 1918 57th Div A+Q (4)

Place	Date	Hour	Summary of Events and Information	Remarks and references to Appendices
W. Ellens	31st		Capt J.H. Orton after Dr Seall Capt 17th Bn Reinforcement division monthly. Infantry 70 Officers 831 OR. R.E. 1 Officer 2 OR. R.A.M.C. 2 Officers 9 OR. OBC 8 OR. AA	AA
			Casualties Officers killed 10, wounded 24, mch 27. Other Ranks	AA
			Killed 115 wounded 642 missing 116 Inguni 18 mch 791 S.I. 3	
			Ktal 1750.	AA
			Dr Staff. Maj-Gr. R.W.R. Barnes CB DSO. ADC's Capt I.B. Jemmer Capt How R.E. Phillipson OBOI Lt.Col J.R. Wethered AAQMG new Is in turn Stone Officer from Capt JF Wathewalt T/Lt W In Stewart DSO Dray Major B.S. Inns-Rhumdu DSO OBE DAQMY T Major J.B. White DSO MC. ADMS Col T. Stewart CB TD. DAPM Capt H.M. Rogers Shahaus 21.	

R.W. Barnes Maj
Maj-Gen
Cmdg 51st Divisn

Army Form C. 2118.

WAR DIARY
INTELLIGENCE SUMMARY.
(Erase heading not required.)

57th Div A & Q
November 1918

WO 22

Place	Date	Hour	Summary of Events and Information	Remarks and references to Appendices
MONS-EN-BAROEUL	November 1		Division moves to rest billets with HQ at Mons-En-Baroeul and troops in Eastern entrefets of LILLE.	
	8		Major (T/Lt-Col) H.W.P. Stokes DSO ASC is appointed A.D. of S.T Bunbury Corps	
			Major W.R. Gibson DSO ASC is appointed to the command of 57 Div Train with Acting rank of Lt-Colonel vice Major (T/Lt-Col) H.W.P. Stokes DSO	
	9		Lieut A.H. Grant MC 3rd Bn South Lancs Regt attached 2/4 Bn South Lancs Regt is appointed Staff Captain 229th Infy Bde with temporary rank of Captain	
	11		Armistice with Germany begins 11:00 hours	
	12		Major C.C. Foss VC DSO Bedford Regt is appointed GSO 1st grade 57th Division with temporary rank of Lt-Colonel vice Bt Lieut-Colonel (T/Lt-Colonel) J.R. Wethered DSO Gloucester Regt to England.	
	21		Major D. Grant-Dalton 2nd Bn W. Yorks Regt is appointed Acting 2 in command of the 2/6 Bn "The King's" (Liverpool Regt)	
	30		Total Reinforcements received during November Officer 40 O/Ranks 1502 Casualties for November - Sick Officers 33 O/Ranks 914. Injured O/Ranks 4.	

WAR DIARY

INTELLIGENCE SUMMARY

Army Form C. 2118.

Place	Date	Hour	Summary of Events and Information	Remarks and references to Appendices
MONS-EN BAROEUL	November 30		Divisional Headquarters Staff. G.O.C. Major-General R. W.R. Barnes C.B. DSO. ADC's Captain J.B. J'armay Captain Hon. P.E. Shelliwin. GSO1 Bt. Lt. Major (T/Lt. Colonel) C.C. Low V.C. DSO. GSO2 Captain (T/Major) B.B. van Shuter DSO MC. GSO3 Lieut (T/Captain) J.P. Wattswath AA & QMG Major (T/Lt. Col) W.M. Stewart DSO. DAAG Major B.S. Moss-Blundell DSO ORE. DAQMG T/Major H.B. White DSO MC ADMS Lt. Colonel (T/Colonel) V.J. Dewar CB AMS. DADMS Captain (T/Major) M.B. King MC RAMC. DADOS T/Captain (A/Major) P.B. Denison MCAOD. DADVS T/Major P.W. Dwyer-Smith AVC. APM Captain H.M. Rogers Shropshire L.I. Senior Chaplain D.G.G. Dept Rev. C.E. Burkitt.	

Amos Blunt
Major & AAG
For Major General
Commanding 59th Division

Army Form C. 2118.

WAR DIARY
or
~~INTELLIGENCE SUMMARY.~~
(Erase heading not required.)

57th Division. A & Q

WR 23 'A'

Place	Date	Hour	Summary of Events and Information	Remarks and references to Appendices
Mons-en-Chaussée	2-12-18		57th Division complete moved to DUISANS area & were accommodated in accordance with location list attached appendix A.	
DUISANS	6/12/18		Major (T/Lt Col) W. M. Stewart DSO ADMS of 57th Divn. to XXII Corps as ADMS.	
do	11-12-18		Major B.S. Moss-Blundell DSO OBE Yorkshire Regt to be ADMS of 57th Divn. T/Capt (T/Major) P.H. Lawless, Gen List, assumed duties as DAAG 57th Divn.	
do	12-12-18		Major (T/Lt Col) C.C. Stapledon, Manchester Regt, assumed command 2/6 K.L.R. Capt C.V. Fisher-Rowe M.C. Grenadier Guards (S.R.) to be Bde Major 172nd Inf. Bde. vice Capt. Gillan T.J.H. app. Bde. Major 147th Inf. Bde.	
do	13/12/18		Capt (T/Major) A.S. St G. Mansergh (R Warwick Regt) assumed duties as 2nd i/c 57th Bn. M.G.C.	
do	28/12/18		Major (T/Lt Col) Flt Drew DSO S.L.R. assumed command of 5th K.L.R. Major (T/Lt Col) Makgill-Crichton-Maitland relinquished command of 5th K.L.R. & proceeded to take over command 2nd Bn Grenadier Gds.	
do	29/12/18		Major P.O.L. Jordan relinquished appointment of CRE 57th Divn.	

WAR DIARY
INTELLIGENCE SUMMARY (2) 57th Divn. A+Q

Army Form C. 2118.

Place	Date	Hour	Summary of Events and Information	Remarks and references to Appendices
SOISSONS	3.12.18		Major Bt/Lt.Col. D.O.B. Dawson S.L.R. resumed command of 1/5 K.N.L.R. vice Lt Col. Goodwin.	
	3.12.18		Major (A/Lt.Col.) J.P. Goodwin relinquished command of 5 K.L.R. resumed duties as CRE 57 Divn. Total reinforcements during month :- Infantry 20 offrs + 538 o.r. R.A. 138 o.r. - R.E. (incl. Signals) 64 o.r. - R.A.M.C. 5 o.r. - 5)' Div Train 51 o.r. - other units 8 o.r. Total sick : 17 offrs 770 o.r. Div HQ Staff : G.O.C. Major Genl. R.W.R. Barnes C.B. D.S.O. A.D.C. Capt. Hon. P.E. Thellusson. Capt I.A. L'ARMAN. G.S.O.1 Capt. R. Thomson (1/L.Col.) C.C. Foss V.C. D.S.O. G.S.O.2 T/Major B. Saxon Bingham D.S.O. M.C. I.T/Capt J.P. Wattleworth Marshall Major M.H.C. A.S. Moss-Blundell D.S.O. O.B.E. DAAG T/Major P.H. Lawless DADMS Capt T/Major N.A. White D.S.O. M.C. A.D.M.S. Col. T.F. Dewar (A) Lt.Col. P. Rutherford DADMS Lt. T/Major M.A. King M.C. DADVS Major P.O. Bayer-Smith DAPD Lt. T/Capt. M.L. Rogers	

Army Form C. 2118.

HQ AG Q 57 D

98 24

WAR DIARY
INTELLIGENCE SUMMARY.
(Erase heading not required.)

Instructions regarding War Diaries and Intelligence Summaries are contained in F.S. Regs., Part II. and the Staff Manual respectively. Title pages will be prepared in manuscript.

Place	Date	Hour	Summary of Events and Information	Remarks and references to Appendices
Duran	1.1.19		Divisional Race Meeting. Area Recommended tactics by Major Bulgeaux attached. Strength total 17 Officers 869 other ranks	
	5.1.19		Sergt. Major B.B. Von in Shum ECO & appointed ADC & Corps 5.1.19. Lt.Col. The Hon. G. Keppel R.F.O. appointed A.D.C. to GOC 5.1.19. Rev. E.H. Beattie M.C. appointed Senior Chaplain vice Major C.B. Burkitt S.C.F. to II Corps as DACG	
	19.1.19		Sergt. Major (a/Lieut-Col) C.L. Macdonald, Manchester Regt appointed to command 2/6 Kings Liverpool Regt vice Lt.Col. C.C. Stapledon to command 2nd Manchester Regt 17.1.19. Lieut Col (a/Brig Col) Stapledon relinquished his temp rank of Colonel	
	21.1.19		Bewer, ADMS, on proceeding to England for demobilization 21.1.19	
	23.1.19		Capt W.O. Ray, N.Z.H.R. Capt. 171 Bde. proceeded to D.M.G's office GHQ 23.1.19	
	27.1.19		Presentation of Colours to the following units took place at Agny en Sucain on 27th Jany 1919, 2/5 Kings Own Lancasters Regt, 2/7 Kings Lipool Regt, 2/4 Rount & Lancs Regt, 2/4 Loyal North Lancs Regt, 2/5 Loyal North Lancs Regt (Pioneers). The Colours were Consecrated by the Right Rev. Bishop Gwynne D.D. Deputy Chaplain General to the Forces at 14.30 hours	

WAR DIARY
INTELLIGENCE SUMMARY

Army Form C. 2118.

Place	Date	Hour	Summary of Events and Information	Remarks and references to Appendices
Divisional	30/1/19		and presented by the G.O.C. 57th Division. The Officer in Command of the Parade was Brig. Gen. A.J. Hanson DSO, M.C, 171st Infantry Brigade.	
	31.1.19		Remainder of Horses demobilised to date 10 199. Demobilised up to 31st Jan 1919 Officers 197 Other ranks Reinforcements for January 2 Officers 252 Other ranks Sick - 11 Officers 371 Other ranks.	
			Div. H.Q. Staff. G.O.C. Major General R.W.R. Barnes CB DSO A.Q. Lt. Col. Hon. G. Rodd. G.S.O.1. Capt. P/Major T/Lt. Col. Rawlins Major DA.A.G. T/Major P.H. Sanders DA.QMG. T/Major W.B. White D.S.O. M.C A/A.D.M.S. a/Lt.Col. P. Rutherford D.A.D.M.S. Lt/T Major M.B. King R.C. D.A.D.V.S. Major R.W. Boyer Junior D.A.P.M. 2nd Lt/(a/Lt H.W. Rogers	

Army Form C. 2118.

WAR DIARY

INTELLIGENCE SUMMARY.
(Erase heading not required.)

HQ ARQ 57 D

	Date	Hour	Summary of Events and Information	Remarks and references to Appendices
DUISANS	Feb'y 1919 9		Bt Major R.V.G. Horn. D.S.O. M.C. Royal Scots Fusiliers appointed G.S.O.2. 57th Division and assumes duty.	
	11		Bt Lt. Colonel R.C. Laurie R.F.A. appointed to command of 285th Bde R.F.A. vice Lt. Col. S.E. Crookes and resumes duty	
	21		Captain & Lt. Colonel A.W.B. Loudon commanding 3/2 West Lancs Field Ambulance proceeds for demobilization	
	23		T/Major N.B. White D.S.O. M.C. General List. DAQMG 57th Division appointed DAQMG to General Haking at SPA and proceeds to SPA	
	24		Captain A/Major M.B. King M.C. DADMS 57th Division proceeds to ETAPLES for duty at No 51 General Hospital	
	27		Major & Lt. Colonel E.C. Lloyd D.S.O. Royal Irish Regt, Commanding 1st Bn Royal Inniskin Fusiliers proceeds to ENGLAND to report personally at the WAR OFFICE	
	28		Lt. Colonel W. Furnivall Commanding 175th (Army) Bde R.F.A is relieved of his command and proceeds to 9th Division for attachment. Casualties for February - Sick 9 Officers and 279 O/Ranks	

WAR DIARY
or
INTELLIGENCE SUMMARY.
(Erase heading not required.)

Army Form C. 2118.

Place	Date	Hour	Summary of Events and Information	Remarks and references to Appendices
DUISANS	Feby 1919	28	Demobilisation during the month proceeded rapidly. Div. H.Q. Staff. G.O.C. Major General R.W.R. BARNES C.B. DSO. ADC to GOC Lt. Colonel Hon G. KEPPEL G.S.O.1. Captain Bt Major JEMPY Lt. Colonel C.C. FOSS V.C. DSO G.S.O.2 Bt Major R.V.G. HORN DSO MC. G.S.O.3 Jempy Captain J.P. WATTLEWORTH AA&QMG Major Jempy Lt. Colonel B.S. MOSS-BLUNDELL DSO. OBE DAAG Jempy Major P.H. LAWLESS MC. A/ADMS Captain a/Lt. Colonel P. RUTHERFORD DADVS Major P.W. DAYER-SMITH DAPM Lieut T/Captain H.M. ROGERS	

M.R.Muslim.
Lieut Colonel
A.A.Y.Q.M.G
For Major General
Commanding 57th Division

WAR DIARY
or
INTELLIGENCE SUMMARY.
(Erase heading not required.)

Army Form C. 2118.

AQ

Jul 26

Place	Date	Hour	Summary of Events and Information	Remarks and references to Appendices
DUISANS	March 1919 15		Major E.H. BEATTIE, M.C. Senior Chaplain (D.C.G.S. Dept.) proceeded for demobilization.	
	19		T/Capt: J.P. WATTLEWORTH (R.F.A.) G.S.O.3 proceeded on leave to U.K.	
	23	0005	57th Divisional Headquarters eliminated on being reduced to Cadre strength. Cadre of Artillery Headquarters affiliated to Div H.Q cadre - the two combined adopting the title :- "Headquarters 57th Divisional Group of Cadres." Major-General R.W.R. BARNES, C.B., D.S.O. (X Hussars) handed over command to J/Brig-General G.C.B. PAYNTER, D.S.O. (Scots Guards) and proceeded to U.K. to report to War Office, accompanied by his A.D.C. Major (Lt-Col.) Hon: G. KEPPEL (R. of O.) Bt.Major R.G.V. HORN, G.S.O.2 (R.Scots Fus) proceeded to 59th Divn as G.S.O.2.	
	24		Major P.W. DAYER-SMITH (AVC) O.B.E. D.A.D.V.S. proceeded for demobilization.	

Army Form C. 2118.

WAR DIARY
or
INTELLIGENCE SUMMARY.
(Erase heading not required.)

Instructions regarding War Diaries and Intelligence Summaries are contained in F. S. Regs., Part II. and the Staff Manual respectively. Title pages will be prepared in manuscript.

Place	Date	Hour	Summary of Events and Information	Remarks and references to Appendices
DUISANS	27		1/Brig-General G. MEYNELL, C.M.G. (Shropshire Light Infantry) assumed command of Div'l Group of Badies on 1/Br-Gen'l G.C.B. PAYNTER, D.S.O. proceeding to U.K. with instructions to report to War office.	
	28		Major (1/Lt-Col) B.S. MOSS-BLUNDELL, D.S.O, O.B.E. (Yorks Regt) proceeded to 3rd Tank Group to take up appointment of D.A.A. & Q.M.G. Headquarter Staff:- 1/Br-Gen'l. G. MEYNELL, C.M.G. G.O.C. 1/Capt: W.G. CAIRD, R.E. A.D.A.Q.M.G. Lieut (1/Capt:) J.H. BRADLEY, M.C. (8th L'pool Regt:) Staff Capt. Lieut. H. WEST, (5th S. Lanc: Regt:) Actg: A.D.C. and Camp Commandant. Major S.F. BURNE, D.S.O. Bde: Major R.A.	

Meynell
Capt SC
+ Brigadier-General,
Comdg. 57½ Div'l Group of Badies.

WAR DIARY

INTELLIGENCE SUMMARY

(Erase heading not required.)

Army Form C. 2118.

HQ 57th Divisional Group of Cadres

AQR

Place	Date	Hour	Summary of Events and Information	Remarks and references to Appendices
DUISANS	1919. Apl. 20th	—	T/Brig-General G. MEYNELL, C.M.G. (Shropshire Light Infantry) proceeded to England to report in writing to War Office, and handed over command of the Divisional Group to Lieut-Colonel D.O.B. DAWSON, 2nd Bn. S. Lanco: Regt. (O.C. 1/5th L.N. Lanco. Regt.) on instructions being received that in future Divisional Groups would be commanded by the Senior Lieut-Colonel present. Headquarter Staff:- Lieut-Colonel D.O.B. DAWSON, (2nd S. Lancs. R.) Cmdg. T/Capt. W.G. CAIRD, R.E. A/D.A.Q.M.G. Lieut. (T/Capt.) J.H. BRADLEY, M.C. (8th L'pool Regt.) Staff Captain. Lieut. (A/Capt.) H. WEST, (5th S. Lanco: Regt.) Actg. A.D.C. and Camp Commandant. Major S.F. BURNE, D.S.O. (16th.) Major R.A.	98 27

D. Dawson
(T/Capt &) Lieut-Colonel,
Cmdg. 57th Divl. Group.

Army Form C. 2118.

WAR DIARY
or
INTELLIGENCE SUMMARY.
(Erase heading not required.)

HQ 54th Divisional Group of Cadres

No. 26

Place	Date	Hour	Summary of Events and Information	Remarks and references to Appendices
Duisans	11/5/19		Cadres of two companies 54th Bn. M.G.C., 2/6 Bn. Kings L'pool Regt. and 2/1 Bn. Kings L'pool Regt. entrained at MAROEUIL for England.	
			In command :- Lt. Col. D.O.B. Dawson 2nd Bn. 5 Lanc att. 1/5-2/14 Lancs.	
			Headquarters Staff Lieut. (1/Capt.) J.H. Bradley MC (8th L'pool Regt.)	
			D.A.A.G., Lieut. (a/Capt.) H. West (5th South Lancs Regt.) a.D.b. and	
			Camp Commandant, Major S.F. Burne D.S.O. Brigade	
			Major R.A.	

Arthur
Lieut. Col.
Comdg. 54th Divisional Group

Army Form C. 2118.

WAR DIARY
or
INTELLIGENCE SUMMARY.
(Erase heading not required.)

AR.11
WAR DIARY 54th Divisional Group of Cadres

Place	Date	Hour	Summary of Events and Information	Remarks and references to Appendices
Louisiana	1/6/19	—	Cadres of 8th Bn. K.L. Regt. remaining 2 boys and 1/4 Bn 54 Bn M.G.C. 2/4 Bn. 1/5 Lancs Regt. departed MAROEVIL for U.K.	
	2/6/19	—	H.Qrs 170th Inf. Bde., 1/5 Bn K.O.R.L. Regt. 1/4 Bn L.N.L. Regt., 1/- Bn. L.N Lancs Regt. 170th L.T.M.B., 1/5 Wessex Fd Amb., No 2 Coy 54th Divl. Train departed from MAROEVIL for U.K. Lt. Col. B.G. Hitchins DSO Comdg 1/5 Btn. L.N.L. Regt. (R.) assumed Command vice Lt. Col. D'O.B. Dawson 1/5 Btn L.N.F. Regt who proceeded to U.K with Cadre of his Unit.	
	3/6/19	—	H.Qrs. Lucknow Inf. C.B., H Qrs 171st Inf. Bde, 1st Royal Munsters, 141st L.T.M B 1/5 W. Lancs. Jn.A. 504 Light Rly Coy R.E. No 3 Coy 54th Divl. Train 2/3 Wessex Fd Amb. 176th + Coy 54th Divl. Train	
	4/6/19	—	9th Btn. K L Regt., 4 Bn 17th Inf Bn. 180 L.T.M.B. 505 Light Coy R.E. 1/5 L.N.L. R.(R) Bavh 54th Divl Sup Ser. Lt. Col L.J. Slitt comdg 51st D.A. to assumed command vice Lt. Col. L.J. Hitchens D.S.O. 1/5 Bn L.N.L.(R) who proceeded to U.K. with cadre of his Unit	

Army Form C. 2118.

WAR DIARY
or
INTELLIGENCE SUMMARY.
(Erase heading not required.)

57 Div. G.S.

Place	Date	Hour	Summary of Events and Information	Remarks and references to Appendices
Duisans	6.6.19	—	H/Qrs 286" Bde R.F.A. & B.C Batteries part D. Batt. departed ACQ for U.K.	
	8.6.19	—	Remainder D/286 Bde R.F.A. remainder 57th Div. Sig Coy, part of 57th D.A.C. departed ACQ for U.K. Major J.H. Barker 255" Bde R.F.A. assumed command vice Lt Col Stitt.	
	25.6.19	—	Remainder 57th D.A.C. x/57th & 3/57th M.T.M. Batts: 2/5th W.L. M.G.B. Vety Sec. and H.Qrs. and H.Qrs. Coy 57th Div Train departed ACQ	
			Div. Staff. Lieut. (T/Capt) J.H. Bradley M.C. (8th Bn Liverpool Regt.) D.A.A.G., (A/Capt) H. West (5th South Lancs Regt.) A.D.C. and Camp Commandant.	

Captain
Staff Captain
57th Divl. Troops

www.ingramcontent.com/pod-product-compliance
Lightning Source LLC
Chambersburg PA
CBHW081440160426
43193CB00013B/2339